LIGHTS OUT?

LIGHTS OUT?

The Outlook for Energy in Eastern Europe and the Former Soviet Union

THE WORLD BANK
Washington, D.C.

© 2010 The International Bank for Reconstruction and Development / The World Bank
1818 H Street NW
Washington DC 20433
Telephone: 202-473-1000
Internet: www.worldbank.org
E-mail: feedback@worldbank.org

1 2 3 4 13 12 11 10

ISBN: 978-0-8213-8296-7
eISBN: 978-0-8213-8297-4
DOI: 10.1596/978-0-8213-8296-7

Cover photo: Otar Jangveladze

Library of Congress Cataloging-in-Publication Data

Lights out? : the outlook for energy in Eastern Europe and the former Soviet Union.
    p. cm.
  Includes bibliographical references and index.
  ISBN 978-0-8213-8296-7 (alk. paper) — ISBN 978-0-8213-8297-4
  1. Energy industries—Europe, Eastern. 2. Energy industries--Former Soviet republics. 3. Energy development—Europe, Eastern. 4. Energy development—Former Soviet republics. I. World Bank.
  HD9502.E832L54 2010
  333.790947—dc22
                                                            2010002471

Contents

Boxes

Figures

Tables

Foreword

Before the current economic crisis hit the Europe and Central Asia (ECA) region in 2008, energy security was a major source of concern in Central and Eastern Europe and in many of the economies in the former Soviet Union. Energy importers were experiencing shortages leading to periodic brownouts and blackouts. An energy crisis seemed imminent.

The unexpected fall in economic activity due to the financial crisis staved off the energy crunch. But this is a temporary reprieve. As economic production begins to grow, the energy hungry economies in the region will again face shortages. This is especially true of ECA's energy importers, who will again be squeezed between their wealthier neighbors to the west and the big oil and gas suppliers in the east.

The countries in the region can avert this potential energy crunch. But given the long lead times associated with most energy investments they need to act now. In addition, they need to act responsibly. This involves pursuing environment-friendly options to manage demand. It involves creating an enabling environment to attract the large investments that are needed. The countries also need to cooperate at the regional level to optimize supply security and cost effectiveness.

This report analyzes the outlook for energy demand and supply in the region. It estimates the investment requirements and highlights the potential environmental concerns associated with meeting future energy needs, including those related to climate change. The report also proposes the actions necessary to create an attractive environment for investment in cleaner energy. Greater regional cooperation for smart energy and climate action is an important part of the World Bank's engagement in Europe and Central Asia. I hope this report will promote a greater understanding of energy sector issues in the region and encourage actions that will improve the lives of people in and around the ECA region.

Philippe Le Houerou
Vice President
Europe and Central Asia Region

Acknowledgments

This report was put together by a team comprising John Besant-Jones, Henk Busz, Franz Gerner, Thomas Hogan, Ranjit Lamech, Arto Nuorkivi, Christian E. Petersen, John Strongman, Gary Stuggins, Claudia Vasquez, and Andrea Zanon. Peter Thomson and Indermit Gill directed and managed the team. Valuable contributions and comments were received from Jane Ebinger, Adriana Eftimie, Peter Johansen, Iftikhar Khalil, Kari Nyman, Dejan Ostojic, Robert P. Taylor, Alexandrina Platonova-Oquab, Pekka Salminen, Gevorg Sargsyan, Michael Stanley, and Bent Svensson. Outside comments from Fatih Birol (International Energy Agency [IEA]), Brendan Devlin (European Commission [EC]), Ann Eggington (IEA), Bernd Kalkum (Consultant), and Jefferey Piper (EC) are gratefully acknowledged. Richard Auty (University of Lancaster) and Marcelo Selowsky (ECA former chief economist) peer reviewed the report.

Rozena Serrano provided administrative support. Barbara Karni edited the book. The World Bank's Office of the Publisher coordinated the design, production, and printing of the book.

Abbreviations

$ All dollar amounts are U.S. dollars unless otherwise indicated.

AAU   assigned amount unit
ACG   Azeri-Chirag-Guneshli
BEEF   Bulgarian Energy Efficiency Fund
CCS   Clinical Center of Serbia
CENEf   Center for Energy Efficiency
CHP   combined heat and power
CIF   Climate Investment Funds
CIS   Commonwealth of Independent States
CMEA   Council for Mutual Economic Assistance
CO_2 carbon dioxide
CSE   Central and Southeastern Europe
CTF   Clean Technology Fund
EIA   Energy Information Administration
ESCO   energy service company
EU   European Union
GDP   gross domestic product
GEF   Global Environmental Facility
GGFR   Global Gas Flaring Reduction
IEA   International Energy Agency

NOx	general oxides of nitrogen
OECD	Organisation for Economic Co-operation and Development
OPEC	Organization of Petroleum Exporting Countries
SCF	Strategic Climate Fund
SOx	general oxides of sulfur
U.K.	United Kingdom

Units

Ktoe	thousand tons of oil equivalent
kWh	kilowatt hour
MtCO2e	carbon dioxide equivalents
Mtoe	million tons of oil equivalent
tCO2e	tons carbon dioxide emissions
TWh	terawatt-hours

Overview

Summary

- Emerging Europe and Central Asia, the region made up of the countries of Central and Eastern Europe (CEE) and the Commonwealth of Independent States (CIS), is a major energy supplier to both Eastern and Western Europe. However, the outlook for both primary and derivative energy supplies is questionable, with a real prospect of a significant decline during the next two decades.

- Western Europe is heavily dependent on energy imports from this region. It will therefore be affected by declines in primary energy supplies. But Western Europe has the financial capacity to secure the energy supplies it needs (albeit at the expense of others). In contrast, the region's energy-importing countries are caught between Western Europe, which has increasing import needs, and the region's exporters, whose exports will likely decline. These countries face the prospect of being squeezed both financially and in terms of energy access.

- This difficult prospect is compounded by the deterioration of the region's energy infrastructure, including power generation and district heating. Although the public sector will have to finance a portion of these investments, it will not have the capacity to meet the full investment needs. It is therefore essential that countries in the region move quickly to put in place an enabling environment to support investment in the sector.

(continued)

Summary

(continued)

- Overlaying all of this are environmental concerns, in particular concern about climate change. Member states of the European Union (EU) and those with EU ambitions will need to meet the challenging EU greenhouse gas emissions targets. At the same time, a number of countries in the region will face the temptation to use environmentally unfriendly technology to meet their immediate energy needs.

- Policy responses need to emphasize demand-side management and the use of energy efficiency measures. The Russian Federation, as the region's major energy exporter, needs to direct additional resources to energy production over the longer term if export levels are to be maintained. Incentives need to be devised and implemented to encourage countries to avoid environmentally unfriendly solutions.

Following the break-up of the Soviet Union, the countries of Central and Southeastern Europe (CSE) and the Commonwealth of Independent States (CIS) experienced six years of dramatic economic decline, starting in 1990. The CEE/CIS region then stagnated for three years, through 1998 until, in 1999, a vigorous economic recovery began for the region as a whole, enabling it to become one of the most economically dynamic in the world. With the onset of the economic and financial crises in 2008, the region's economic performance experienced a sharp reversal, with economic declines that were among the largest in the world.

This economic performance was reflected in the region's energy sector. The initial economic decline was accompanied by a sharp reduction in the production and consumption of energy. Maintenance and upgrading of the stock of energy assets became an early investment casualty of the economic decline. As the region's economy recovered, both production and consumption increased. However, the deterioration in the asset base and the associated loss of both capacity and efficiency proved such that by the end of 2007, a number of countries in the region were experiencing periodic energy shortages, and a serious energy crunch appeared imminent.

The rapid rise in energy prices in 2008 followed by the onset of the financial and economic crises dampened demand significantly, creating some breathing room before energy availability again becomes a serious concern. But this is only a temporary respite. Energy prices have moderated, and the assumption in this report is that although significant price volatility will continue to be the norm, prices will average out at a level close to long-run marginal cost. In the case of oil, this is estimated to be $60–$70 a barrel in 2008 dollar terms.

TABLE 1

Average Annual Growth Projections for GDP, Electricity Consumption, and Primary Fuel Consumption in the Region, 2005–30

Item	Annual growth (percent)
GDP	4.4
Electricity consumption	3.1
Primary fuel consumption	1.9

Source: World Bank staff calculations.

Although the region has been hit hard by the crisis, focused efforts are being directed at mitigating the impact, with the objective of avoiding another "lost decade." Nonetheless, the expectation is that the region as a whole will recover to the 2008 level of output only by 2013. There are reasonable prospects that, with policy reforms, the region as a whole can expect a resumption of long-term average economic growth of almost 5 percent a year after 2011. This translates into an average growth rate for the period 2005–30 of 4.4 percent a year. The assumption of a 4.4 percent growth rate results in an expected annual increase in electricity consumption of about 3.1 percent and an annual increase in primary fuel consumption of about 1.9 percent (table 1).

The Energy Supply Outlook

The region is a major energy supplier to both Eastern and Western Europe. But the outlook for increasing primary energy supplies is not promising, with a real prospect for a decline over the next 20–25 years. There is also the prospect of a shift in primary energy supplies. Concern about gas availability and a political push toward supplier diversification could increase both reliance on coal—more polluting but locally available—and resistance to shutting down aging nuclear reactors.

The demand for primary energy in the region is expected to increase by 50 percent over 2005 levels by 2030. The underlying resource base has the capacity to meet at least a portion of this increase, provided adequate funds are directed to the upstream sectors. However, in the case of oil, unless substantial new discoveries are made, the region's oil production could peak in the next 10–15 years and then start to decline, although the decline could be delayed if investment in the Russian Federation were to increase significantly. For gas, unless Russia, the dominant producer, mobilizes the needed funding and technology to develop its known gas deposits and associated infrastructure, production is likely to plateau in the next 15–20 years. Increased investment could delay the onset of the production plateau (box 1).

BOX 1.

Proposed Russian Gas Exports to China

On October 14, 2009, during Russian Prime Minister Vladimir Putin's visit to Beijing, Russia reportedly entered into an agreement with China for the future supply of 68 billion cubic meters a year of gas.

It will be interesting to see how Russia supplies these additional volume. Just to maintain gas production levels in Russia, Gazprom would need to invest about $15 billion a year. To meet potential increases in demand, capital investment would have to increase to $20 billion a year. Between 2001 and 2008, however, Gazprom's capital investments for upstream gas exploration and development totaled about $36 billion, according to Gazprom financial statements. Although capital spending increased between 2006 and 2008, it remains below the required level ($8.6 billion was spent in 2008, according to Gazprom's financial statements).

In the absence of an increase in production, a reduction in domestic demand would free up additional supplies for export. Also, Russia has been purchasing gas from the Central Asian producers, primarily Turkmenistan.

Many of the countries in the region have domestic coal resources that can be developed. Exploitation of these resources, however, will conflict with growing concerns about greenhouse gas emissions and their impact on climate change. These concerns will limit the extent to which domestic coal will substitute for oil and gas in Member countries of the European Union (EU) and countries with EU membership aspirations, although some of these countries may increasingly turn to nuclear power as an alternative. Other countries, however, will be tempted to use environmentally unfriendly technology to meet their immediate energy needs.

If primary energy production is to be maintained or increased, significant investment will be required. The projected needs for primary energy development for 2010–30 are estimated at almost $1.3 trillion. While these funds are expected to be available in Russia and other oil- and gas-producing countries in the region, they must be targeted to develop the necessary upstream production facilities, transportation infrastructure, and refinery capacity to meet Europe's primary energy requirements. Governments will have to transfer responsibilities for operation, maintenance, rehabilitation, and investment from state budgets to state-owned or private enterprises and facilitate their operation on commercial lines. Prices should be market based and aim at full cost recovery. Under these conditions, internal cash flow would be adequate to support the required program of investment.

Without such targeted investments, primary energy supplies will decline. Western Europe, which is heavily dependent on energy imports from the region, will be affected by declines in primary energy supplies. But countries in Western Europe have the financial means to secure their energy needs, albeit at the expense of other countries. The CSE/CIS energy-importing countries will be squeezed between Western Europe, with its increasing import needs, and the region's exporters, whose exports will likely decline.

Compounding these difficulties is the region's deteriorating energy infrastructure, especially for power generation and district heating (box 2). The region's power infrastructure is in desperate need of upgrading. Electricity capacity in the region has barely increased since

---

BOX 2.

Business Concerns about Electricity Supply

The fourth World Bank/European Bank for Reconstruction and Development Business Environment and Enterprise Performance Survey (BEEPS)—conducted in 2008, before the onset of the financial and economic crises—shows that electricity supply is a major concern to businesses throughout the region. In Albania, for example, electricity supply is the top concern for businesses of all sizes and types. Widespread electricity supply disruptions over the past few years have prompted many businesses to invest in back-up diesel generators, which are expensive to operate and maintain. Their excessive use during blackouts contributes heavily to local air and noise pollution.

The 2008 survey shows a dramatic increase in concerns about electricity supply since the previous survey, conducted in 2005. In every country surveyed, the percentage of firms that considered electricity supply a problem rose, in many cases dramatically. The legacy of abundant electricity infrastructure that characterized the first decade and a half of transition had disappeared by 2008.

BOX TABLE

Percentage of Firms that Consider Electricity a Problem in Doing Business

Subregion	BEEPS 2005	BEEPS 2008
Europe and Central Asia Region	17	47
EU-10 (Central Europe)	11	41
Southeastern Europe	26	48
CIS North	9	58
CIS South	21	51

Source: World Bank and EBRD 2008.

the early 1990s, and plants are getting old. Most thermal plants, especially coal-fired plants, pollute well above EU standards, use fuel inefficiently, and operate unreliably (box 3). The deteriorating capacity has not yet become a full-blown crisis, because of the decline in demand during the 1990s and the current drop-off in demand related to the economic crisis. But construction lead times of several years mean that action is required now.

About $1.5 trillion in investment is needed in the power sector over the next 20–25 years, and another $500 billion is required for district heating. Total energy investment requirements in the region thus amount to almost $3.3 trillion, or about 3 percent of cumulative GDP (table 2). This level of investment cannot be provided in the region by the public sector alone. Attracting private sector investors will require improving the investment climate to make it conducive to such investment.

BOX 3.

The 2006 Disaster in Alchevsk, Ukraine

Many Ukrainian families rely on district heating, and district heating accounts for a large share of energy consumption in Ukraine. But low tariffs have prevented district heating companies from making critically needed investments for maintenance and upgrading. About 70 percent of the Ukrainian district heating system is in need of renovation. This means that many systems are not only in financial trouble but also at high risk for outages and technical failures.

On January 22, 2006, the worst-case scenario was dramatically demonstrated when the district heating system in Alchevsk, a town of 120,000 people in southeastern Ukraine, collapsed. The winter was very cold, with temperatures dropping to –30°C. When a boiler failure was not repaired quickly, the main district heating pipes froze and the system collapsed within several hours. The damage was extensive—almost all the pipes were damaged—and there was little room for substituting alternative energy sources. As a result, hundreds of buildings, including schools and hospitals, were cut off from the heating system and left to rely on individual electric heaters.

The vulnerable population—about 4,500 children and elderly people—was evacuated to southern Ukraine, where they were put up in hotels and other facilities. Until the spring, the city of Alchevsk was largely deserted, with only a few residential areas and businesses able to function. The entire system had to be replaced, at significant expense to the government, in a nationally declared emergency.

TABLE 2

Projected Energy Sector Investment Needed in the Region by 2030–35

(billions of dollars)

Sector	Investment required
Crude oil	900
Refining	20
Gas	230
Coal	150
Electricity	1,500
Heating	500
Total	3,300

Source: World Bank staff calculations.

The Outlook for Regional Cooperation

Regional cooperation on electricity production and gas transport is needed to boost supply security and cut costs. The driving factors are the large mismatches between supply and demand between countries and the uneven concentration of resources, especially the focus on supply from Russia. Committing to international trade offers substantial potential for confronting the region's huge needs for investing in new capacity. It enables interconnected power systems to work as one larger system, capturing economies of scale with joint planning and implementation for capacity additions and coordinated dispatch of generating plants. A major issue for electricity trade is dealing with the risks for investments in new supply capacity and the risks for supply security. Most countries in the region have yet to develop the institutional arrangements to manage such risks.

In Southeastern Europe, for example, countries that plan to rely on gas-fired power-generating capacity must be confident that other countries will also follow this regional priority, rather than pursue self-sufficiency in generating capacity through non gas sources. Otherwise, the base load will not be sufficient to justify the large investments required in gas transmission systems. But many countries have announced plans to build new generating capacity without a gas-fired component—not a promising development for gas supply infrastructure in the subregion. Such large regional commitments require that gas supplies be assured, something that is uncertain in both the near and long terms.

Central Asia has considerable potential for exporting electricity—within its boundaries and beyond—but the prospects for realizing this potential are uncertain, because of the long history of distrust among countries and their lack of institutional and financial capacity. Water and hydropower politics are deeply intertwined. Irrigation water is needed in the summer; electricity is needed more in the winter.

The Central Asian Regional Economic Cooperation (CAREC) is helping coordinate matters. Two changes are needed for success: regional cooperation and government willingness to create a business climate that attracts the huge investments required. These conditions are vital for ensuring adherence to contract commitments (including payments), stopping side deals that undermine investment viability, and countering the prevailing nonperformance of obligations.

The Outlook for Reducing Waste

The countries in the region waste too much energy in production and transmission, especially through gas flaring and venting. Some flaring and venting is needed to ensure safe operation. But most associated gas is flared and vented because there is no infrastructure or market to use the gas, leaving it stranded. And because of the relative demand for oil and gas, operators have little incentive to delay oil production to find uses for the associated gas.

Russia is the largest gas flarer in the world, flaring and venting 55 billion cubic meters of associated gas in 2005, according to estimates by the World Bank Global Gas Flaring Reduction public-private partnership (box 4). During the same period, Kazakhstan flared and

---

BOX 4.

Reducing Waste in Russia

Satellite images of the earth at night are sometimes used to map the world's economic geography. The lights identify human settlements, illuminating the parts of the world where wealth is concentrated. Satellites over Russia can also identify waste. Gas flaring shows up as brightly lit areas in sparsely populated parts of the country.

One of these parts is near Gubkinsky City, in the Yamal-Nenets Autonomous District in Western Siberia, where the Associated Gas Recovery Project for the Komsomolskoye Oil Field processes gas that would otherwise be flared at the Komsomolskoye oil field. With revenues provided by the Carbon Fund for Europe, the Danish Carbon Fund, the Italian Carbon Fund, and the Spanish Carbon Fund, the project developer will be able to implement a technical solution that allows full utilization of the previously flared gas.

One of the first joint implementation projects in Russia aimed at reducing gas flaring, the project is expected to deliver emission reductions of 6.6 million tons of carbon dioxide equivalent between 2010 and 2012. The four funds will purchase 5.3 $MtCO_2e$ reductions. The project is also expected to deliver about 2 billion cubic meters a year of consumer-grade dry gas to Gazprom plus about 23,000 tons of petroleum liquids.

Source: World Bank 2008a.

vented 8.8 billion cubic meters, putting it fifth worldwide. Azerbaijan, Turkmenistan, and Uzbekistan together flared and vented 7 billion cubic meters of associated gas. Piped natural gas trades at $150 to more than $300 per thousand cubic meters, putting the annual value of the region's gas flared and vented at $10–$20 billion. The region's 70 billion cubic meters a year of wasted gas could provide feedstock for 70 gigawatts of combined-cycle gas turbine plants. In 2006, gas flares in the five countries alone contributed 165 million tons of carbon dioxide equivalents ($MtCO_2e$) into the atmosphere. During the same period, they vented 88 $MtCO_2e$, for a total of 253 $MtCO_2e$ in emissions.

Gas is lost not only during production in fields such as Komsomolskoye. Technical and commercial gas transmission and distribution losses are also high. In Russia, for example, the International Energy Agency estimated in 2005 that 3 percent (or 5.3 billion cubic meters) of the gas distributed through medium- and low-pressure pipelines is leaked into the atmosphere, equivalent to 80 $MtCO_2e$.

These losses cost money and harm the environment. To reduce gas flaring and leakages, governments of oil- and gas-exporting countries can take the following steps:

- Provide guidelines and incentives to state-owned and private companies to capture unused gas that would otherwise be flared, prevent and repair gas pipeline and oil storage leakages, and reduce gas losses through theft and inadequate or absent metering.

- Open oil and gas pipelines to independent producers, including to associated gas from oil producers.

The Outlook for Energy Efficiency

Investing in energy efficiency achieves three goals simultaneously and at least cost: it reduces greenhouse gas emissions, improves energy security, and contributes to more sustainable economic growth. Energy efficiency is thus a triple win for governments, end users, market participants (public and private), and society in general. An additional $1 invested in energy efficiency may avoid more than $2 in supply-side investment. Energy efficiency should therefore be considered as an energy resource, on a par with—and even preferred to—supply-side resources. Much potential remains untapped because of the many obstacles to investments in energy efficiency: inadequate energy prices and lack of payment discipline, insufficient information on suitable technologies, too few contractors and service companies, and financing constraints.

Governments have a major role to play in energy efficiency (box 5). Of course, they must allow energy tariffs to reflect costs. But they must also be proactive in setting and updating energy efficiency standards for homes, equipment, and vehicles—and in enforcing them. Few consumers will take action on energy efficiency on their own; the issue is not significant enough to them. Equipment choices should therefore be limited to equipment with optimal energy efficiency characteristics. To set an example, governments should undertake energy efficiency programs in the public sector, disseminating the results through long-term information campaigns. Doing so would stimulate consumer interest and help develop an energy efficiency industry. Designing cities with alternative means of transportation in mind is another important way for governments to raise energy efficiency.

BOX 5.

Improving Energy Efficiency in Belarus

Belarus relies heavily on the import of primary energy resources, and it imports some electricity. Russia is the main source of these energy imports. In an effort to reduce its dependence on imported energy, the government of Belarus has placed high priority on increasing energy efficiency. Its role in designing and enforcing a comprehensive policy on energy efficiency is one of the main reasons behind the remarkable reduction in the amount of energy consumed per unit of production.

Energy intensity in Belarus decreased by almost 50 percent between 1996 and 2008. The main elements of this success story include the following:

- Establishing energy efficiency institutions with a clear mandate. A Committee for Energy Efficiency was established in 1993 with a mandate to develop and implement the energy efficiency improvement strategy. This committee evolved into the Energy Efficiency Department of the Committee of Standardization, which has pursued a number of countrywide educational campaigns, including awareness raising through television, radio, print media, and special courses for state officials, decision makers, and students.

- Allocating adequate financial resources to implement energy efficiency measures. The financing of energy efficiency measures increased from $47.7 million in 1996 to $1,213.9 million in 2008. Over this period, total investments in energy efficiency amounted to about $4.2 billion.

- Continuing political commitment on the part of the government. The first national energy efficiency program—the National Program for Energy Savings to Year 2000—was approved in 1996. The second national energy efficiency program, for 2001–06, was approved in 2001; the third, for 2006–10, was approved in 2006. The Law on Energy Savings was introduced in 1998.

Globally, the technical potential for better energy efficiency through 2030 is greatest in construction (30 percent reduction), followed by industry (21 percent) and transport (17 percent). Reliable estimates for the region are not yet available, but given the region's generally poor record on energy efficiency, its potential is believed to be much higher. Modernizing district heating networks on densely built areas, rehabilitating combined heat and power plants, and building new plants would reduce total primary energy consumption by 17 percent, or 860 $MtCO_2e$, by 2030.

Commercial banks are ideal vehicles for energy efficiency financing, but banks in the region have shown limited interest in this line of business. The experience of several member countries of the Organisation for Economic Co-operation and Development (OECD) shows that a dedicated energy efficiency fund is essential, both as an originator of bankable projects and as a lender of last resort. Energy service companies specializing in implementing energy efficiency projects are a good solution for large energy consumers (the public sector, industry, and pooled residential projects), but they require sophisticated clients and a good legal and contractual framework. There is a broad range of business models for energy service companies; countries should assess which have the most potential for their market.

Utility demand-side management programs have worked well in some OECD countries where the regulatory framework provides the proper incentives. Together with integrated resource planning and electronic markets, utility demand-side management deserves a new look. It is one of the quickest and most effective ways to boost energy efficiency, especially in reaching small consumers with standard solutions—say, through efficient lighting and appliance replacement programs.

The Outlook for Addressing Climate Change

Although consensus is not complete, many signs point to accelerating global climate change. The impact could be severe, even with immediate and drastic measures to abate emissions.

Greenhouse gas emissions in the Europe and Central Asia region fell during the 1990s, as economic production declined. But with economic recovery in the 2000s, emissions rose again until the economic crisis of 2008. The current slowdown in economic activity will provide only temporary respite. Carbon emissions in the region relative to GDP are among the highest in the world. In 2005 Russia was the third-largest CO_2 emitter in the world, after the United States and China. The region's EU members—despite their reliance on domestic coal—have already started tackling climate change, improving energy efficiency, developing renewable energy technologies, and tapping into carbon finance. Other countries in the region will face increasing pressure to catch up—and quickly.

There is a disconnect between global efforts to reduce carbon emissions and the region's national energy strategies for the next 20 years. The region's policymakers and businesses will have to rethink these strategies and engage seriously in global efforts. Demands for carbon reductions will only intensify. The countries of the region must do their share, but transitioning to a low-carbon economy can be costly. By tapping into carbon finance, countries in the region can reduce their carbon footprint and attract critical capital to rebuild their energy infrastructure and industrial base using efficient and cleaner technologies.

The Kyoto Protocol and the development of the carbon trading market have created instruments to leverage investments in greenhouse gas reductions: project-based carbon financing, the cap-and-trade EU Energy Trading Scheme, the International Emission Trading scheme, and trading of assigned amount units (rights to emit). All could provide big opportunities for countries in the region. Governments should ensure that national policies and legislation facilitate these instruments, foster rapid technological modernization, and spur a revolution toward energy efficiency. In addition, carbon taxes and standards-setting can create incentives for corporations and consumers to change (box 6).

Putting a price on carbon emission makes alternative energy sources viable. The region's large contribution to global warming reflects its high energy and high carbon intensity. The causes? Outmoded generation technology and reliance on coal. Fuel switching means replacing high-carbon fuels with low-carbon fuels. Energy efficiency measures for buildings, transportation, heating, cooling, lighting systems, and so on pay off no matter what the carbon price is. The cost of alternative energy—wind, solar, biomass, and geothermal—is falling. The switch is already taking place in Central and Eastern Europe, where the joint implementation provisions of the Kyoto Protocol have catalyzed renewable energy projects. In general terms, though, the region's renewable energy development is underfunded, and several governments remain unpersuaded of the profitability of renewable energy projects or the environmental benefit deriving from such projects.

BOX 6.

Climate Action in Turkey's Landfills

Not long ago, visitors driving into Turkey's capital city of Ankara from the airport were assaulted by a horrible smell from the decomposing waste at the Mamak landfill alongside the highway. The residues caused environmental and social problems, including air pollution and health risks.

With financing support from the World Bank through the Industrial Development Bank of Turkey (TSKB), the landfill was converted into a garbage-recycling station that creates heat and energy for local greenhouses. A biodigester at the facility treats organic waste and produces biogas. Gas from a landfill gas recovery system and from the biodigester is then used to generate power and heat in a power plant with 14.6 MW of capacity—enough to power 31,000 households in Turkey. Recyclable waste such as glass and plastics are processed and sold. What remains is less than 10 percent of the incoming waste mass, which is placed back in landfills. The landfill, now covered with soil, is being reforested. The excess heat generated by power generation and waste processing is fed to a greenhouse in which tomatoes are grown. Heat will also be provided to a new café on the site.

People living in the area have experienced a big improvement in the quality of life. The rehabilitated landfill no longer poses a health hazard; it has become a generator of both power and local jobs. The project also contributes to the global imperative of climate action by reducing methane gas and carbon dioxide emissions and producing renewable energy.

The Outlook With Higher Energy Prices

Energy prices have been subject to significant volatility over the past several years. Overall, however, the oil- and gas-producing countries in the region have enjoyed the benefits of prices above historic averages (in constant dollar terms). The downside to this, however, is that many resource-rich economies have suffered from a "resource curse" that includes oil price volatility, Dutch disease, deterioration of political systems and state institutions, and underinvestment in human capital. The evidence suggests an adverse impact of resource abundance on long-term growth, but prudent fiscal policies and progressive institutional mechanisms may have provided some protection to producing countries in the region, so far. Wise management of oil revenues requires sustainable public spending to preserve intergenerational equity and macroeconomic stability. A well-functioning and transparent governance framework covering the entire value chain is central to sustaining oil prosperity.

Although rising incomes dramatically reduced poverty in the last decade, inequality is growing in the region, and the current economic and financial crises, coupled with higher energy and food prices, have increased the risk of poverty and vulnerability (box 7). Utility access, quality, and affordability have improved since the 1990s, particularly

---

BOX 7.

The Potential Impact of Higher Energy Prices

Establishing cost-recovery tariffs is key to ensuring the financial viability of energy enterprises. However, it can also generate adverse consequences. For example, as residential tariffs are increased to cost-recovery levels, households, particularly in low-income groups, may switch to cheaper traditional fuels, such as wood, peat, and coal, which contribute to indoor and outdoor air pollution. Although there are no comprehensive data on household emissions, survey evidence indicates that in the wake of higher prices, households do substitute fuels if an effective social protection system is not in place.

Armenia

A survey undertaken in Armenia in the early 2000s (World Bank 2007a) showed that 80 percent of households and 95 percent of poor households reported using alternative fuel sources (primarily wood) in response to rising energy prices. The increased reliance on wood was particularly acute among the urban poor. When asked if they made an effort to reduce their reliance on electricity over the previous 12 months, about 65 percent of the poor and 54 percent of the nonpoor said they had, with the effort highest among the rural poor (71 percent). Although the inefficient practice of heating with electricity has declined, increased wood consumption has created potential environmental problems, such as deforestation and increased air pollution.

Turkey

In the 1980s, natural gas began being supplied to Ankara, reducing pollution in the city. In contrast, Istanbul remained dependent on lignite for heat and thermal power generation. The city was classified by the British Foreign Office as the second most polluted duty station for British diplomats (Mexico City was the most polluted).

With the introduction of natural gas to Istanbul, the city dropped in rank. In recent years, however, as natural gas prices have increased, the use of lignite has started to increase and pollution levels have risen.

in electricity and gas coverage in low-income countries—but these gains are now at risk, particularly if countries elect not to invest in critically needed maintenance activities. Many households continue to use dirty fuels, because coverage and reliability problems persist. Fuel prices need to be set at market levels if investment is to take place, but raising them may push energy prices out of the reach of the poor and vulnerable. Lifeline tariffs, burden limits, and earmarked and nonearmarked cash transfers have all proven effective in aiding the poor. In addition to these social protection instruments, governments in the region should bring their legislation, regulations, procedures, and practices in line with good international practices of social mitigation.

The Outlook for a Better Investment Climate

The total projected energy sector investment requirements for the region over the next 20–25 years are huge—about $3.3 trillion in 2008 dollars, or some 3 percent of accumulated GDP over the period. Although the public sector in these countries will clearly have to finance a portion of these investments, it will not have the capacity to meet the full investment needs. The countries in the region will therefore need to call on the financial depth and technical know-how of private sector investors and energy companies. Although the current financial crisis is a serious impediment to private sector investment in any activities or countries seen as high risk, as the financial crisis passes, the prospects for such investment will improve. However, in order to attract these investors, countries will need to create enabling environments that provide secure ownership rights, are subject to the rule of law, foster transparency, and enable reasonable risk mitigation. In addition, individual sectors will have to be viewed as financially and commercially viable. This will be particularly critical in those sectors, such as electricity and heat, that are largely dependent on their domestic markets (box 8).

In order to create an attractive environment for investment, countries will need to adhere to 10 key principles (box 9). Although these principles are not equally important, all have significant bearing on perceptions of the overall climate for investment. Government actions that are consistent with these principles will go a long way toward creating an attractive and competitive investment climate in the energy sector.

BOX 8.

Addressing Payment Discipline in the Electricity Sector

One of the key challenges for utility companies operating in the region, particularly in the former Soviet republics, has been finding ways to improve payment discipline. The following are anecdotal examples of some of the approaches that have been taken.

Tractabel in Kazakhstan

In the mid-1990s, Tractabel acquired the electricity distribution assets in Almaty, Kazakhstan. In the first six months of operation, the company succeeded in increasing payment levels from less than 30 percent to more than 90 percent, through a ruthless approach to cutting off supply for nonpayment that included cutting off the Ministry of Finance in the middle of a presentation by the minister to potential foreign investors. Tractabel also reportedly became the most unpopular company in Kazakhstan. It subsequently had difficulties in agreeing to the interpretation of the contractual tariff policy. The company's involvement in Kazakhstan was ultimately resolved when the government agreed to buy back the assets.

AES in Georgia

In the late 1990s, AES acquired the Telasi distribution company (covering Tbilisi) and the Gardebani power plant in Georgia. The company had enormous difficulties enforcing payment discipline. At one point, after bills had not been paid for electricity supplied to the presidential palace, AES threatened to cut off supply right before a scheduled visit of a senior European dignitary. The presidential administration pleaded with AES not to cut off supply, and AES accommodated the request. However, the bill remained unpaid, and AES again threatened to cut off supplies. This time the plea was to hold off pending the visit of James Wolfensohn, then president of the World Bank. This time AES was not accommodating. The bill was paid the next day. AES eventually sold out to RAO UES of Russia, which has also struggled with payments.

USAID in Georgia

USAID funded a management contract for the distribution operations of United Energy Distribution Company (UDC) in Georgia. The contract was assigned to PA Consulting, which established meter connections to villages and small towns and then advised local leaders and residents that it was their collective responsibility to make their payments. If payments were made on time, UDC promised 24/7 supply. The approach proved to be very effective, paving the way for UDC privatization to the Czech company CEZ.

BOX 9.

Seven Do's and Three Don'ts for Creating a Better Investment Climate

1. Don't impose a punitive or regressive tax regime.
2. Do introduce an acceptable legal framework.
3. Do provide supporting regulations administered by an independent and impartial regulator.
4. Do create an environment that facilitates assured nondiscriminatory access to markets.
5. Don't interfere with the functioning of the market place.
6. Don't discriminate among investors.
7. Do honor internationally accepted standards.
8. Do abide by contractual undertakings and preclude the use of an administrative bureaucracy to constrain investor activities.
9. Do prevent monopoly abuses.
10. Do ensure that the sector is kept free of corruption.

Given the long lead times required to implement projects in the energy sector, countries need to position themselves to secure funding support for such progress as quickly as they can. Failure to introduce an enabling environment to support investment in the sector will translate into a shortfall in investment that, in turn, could constrain economic activity. A 10 percent shortfall in energy availability could lead to a 1 percent reduction in economic growth; a larger shortfall could have even more detrimental impacts. Time is of the essence.

CHAPTER 1

Introduction

Almost 20 years have passed since the transition process began in the countries of Central and South East Europe (CSE) and the Commonwealth of Independent States (CIS).[1] This transition can be characterized as reflecting three transitions rolled into one:

- A political transition, from a highly controlled centralized political system to a more decentralized and democratic form of government (in some countries this was combined with conflict and political disintegration)

- An institutional transition, from the institutional framework of central planning toward the institution of a market economy

- An economic transition, involving the disintegration of the highly integrated economic space of the former Soviet Union and the Council for Mutual Economic Assistance (CMEA/COMECON), with resultant disruptions in trade, financial, and labor market connections.

In each of these areas, there were broadly two stages of transition. The first was one of economic decline, involving the disintegration and destruction of existing political, institutional, and economic relations (figure 1.1). It was followed by recovery, involving rebuilding, reform, and integration with the world economy (recently, this stage has been affected by the global financial and economic crises).

FIGURE 1.1

Changes in Real Output in the Region, 1990–2008

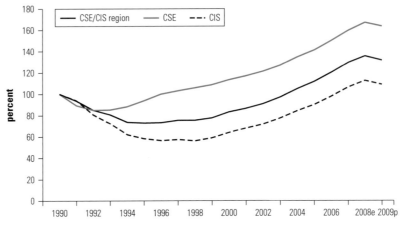

Source: World Bank data base and staff projection.

The region overall initially experienced six years of dramatic economic decline, starting in 1990, during which it lost a third of its measured GDP. It then stagnated for another three years, through 1998. Then, in 1999, a vigorous economic recovery began for the region as a whole. Taking advantage of access to global markets, the region subsequently experienced a rate of growth through 2007 that made it one of the most economically dynamic regions in the world. With the onset of the global financial and economic crises in 2008, the region's economic performance experienced a sharp reversal, with economic declines that were among the highest in the world.

This economic performance has been closely reflected in the region's energy sector. The initial economic decline was accompanied by a sharp reduction in both the production and consumption of energy. Primary energy production dropped steadily through 2000, to about 77 percent of its 1990 levels (figure 1.2). Since then it has increased, reaching 99 percent of its 1990 levels in 2008.

Consumption fell off even more sharply, dropping to 70 percent of 1990 levels in 1999 (figure 1.3). With the economic recovery that got underway at that time, consumption began to increase, but, given improvements in the level of energy intensity, consumption was still at only 80 percent of 1990 levels in 2008. This resulted in a steady growth in exports of primary energy (largely oil and gas), following an initial decline at the beginning of the transition period.

These trends suggest that the region should be amply endowed with energy supply. However, during the economic decline in the early part of the transition period, maintenance and upgrading of

FIGURE 1.2

Primary Energy Production in the Region, by Type, 1990–2008

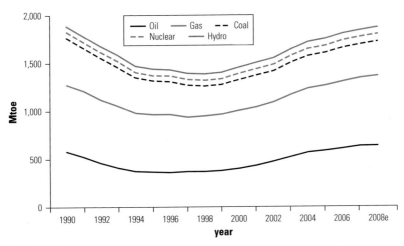

Source: BP 2008.

FIGURE 1.3

Primary Energy Consumption in the Region, 1990–2008

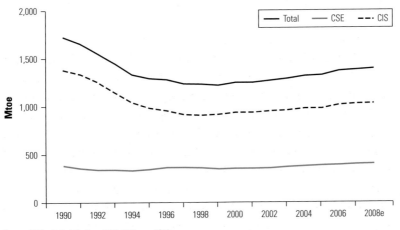

Source: BP Statistical Review of World Energy 2008.

what had come to appear to be oversized infrastructure stock became an early investment casualty. The consequence was a steady deterioration in this stock of assets. At the time, the impact was minimal, but the deterioration in the asset base and the associated loss of both capacity and efficiency became an increasing concern as the economic recovery progressed. By the end of 2007, a number of countries in the region were experiencing periodic energy shortages, and a serious energy crunch appeared highly likely in the relatively near term.

The rapid rise in energy prices in 2008 followed by the onset of the financial and economic crises served to dampen energy demand significantly, creating some breathing room before energy availability again becomes a serious concern. But this is only a temporary respite—and one that may be truncated if governments do not accord adequate priority to asset preservation in allocating investment funds from a more limited envelope.

The disintegration of the highly integrated space of the former Soviet Union and the CMEA has also had an impact on the energy sector in the region. At the beginning of the transition period, the energy sectors of the various countries were heavily interdependent. The energy exporters (the Russian Federation and the Central Asian countries) relied on the energy-importing countries in the region as outlets for their primary fuel exports and, in a number of cases, as transit routes to access markets in Western Europe. The energy importers, in turn, were heavily dependent on Russia and, to a lesser extent, the Central Asian exporters for their primary energy supplies. In addition, within the region, supply chains had been designed to take advantage of the relative endowments of the various energy producers. Thus, in Central Asia, Kazakhstan, Turkmenistan, and Uzbekistan had been suppliers of oil and gas to the subregion, while the Kyrgyz Republic and Tajikistan had exported their surplus hydropower within the region.

Following the break-up of the Soviet Union, the focus steadily switched from an emphasis on optimization of energy production and distribution at the regional level to an emphasis on greater self-sufficiency at the individual country level. At the same time, energy exporters started to explore options to penetrate markets outside the region, while energy importers started looking at different supplier options for portions of their demand. The combination of these factors has resulted in some disintegration of the regional energy homogeneity that had existed in the region at the start of the transition period. Notwithstanding this, however, the region continues to experience considerable energy sector interdependence, which provides a basis for continuing to look at the energy outlook for the region as a whole while recognizing that, at the margin, countries are increasingly looking at options that will reduce this level of interdependence.

The current economic and financial crises have pushed some energy security concerns out of the limelight (although the issue of gas supply to Europe delivered via Ukraine remains very much a concern), but they remain key issues for countries in the region. Energy security, however, is an issue that requires a global response. An international agenda can perhaps best be developed by focusing on three pillars: energy efficiency; diversification of energy supplies, in terms of both the source of supply and diversification among fuels; and strategies to manage price volatility. The challenge for individual countries in the region is how best to adapt their own energy strategies to incorporate these three pillars.

The impact of energy consumption on the environment is also an increasing concern, particularly for EU member countries and countries with EU aspirations that face the prospect of EU–mandated targets for 2020, which call for a 20 percent reduction in carbon emissions compared with 2005 and a 20 percent increase in the use of renewable energy by 2020. Environmental concerns have increased interest in nuclear power and intensified the emphasis on renewable energy sources.

The individual countries and the region as a whole are confronted with an energy outlook fraught with considerable uncertainties. But notwithstanding both these uncertainties and the current economic and financial situation, decisions will have to be made. These decisions will have long-term ramifications and may substantially affect the economic outlook at both the country and the regional level. It is, therefore, incumbent on policy makers to accord these decisions a considerable level of prioritization.

Notes

1. The countries covered are Albania, Armenia, Azerbaijan, Belarus, Bosnia and Herzegovina, Bulgaria, Croatia, the Czech Republic, Estonia, FYR Macedonia, Georgia, Hungary, Kazakhstan, Kosovo, the Kyrgyz Republic, Latvia, Lithuania, Moldova, Montenegro, Poland, Romania, the Russian Federation, Serbia, the Slovak Republic, Slovenia, Tajikistan, Turkey, Turkmenistan, Ukraine, and Uzbekistan (sometimes referred to collectively as Europe and Central Asia).

CHAPTER 2

The Impending
Energy Crunch

At the end of 2007, the Central and South East Europe/ Commonwealth of Independent States (CSE/CIS) countries faced the prospect of an imminent energy crunch, brought on by the convergence of steadily rising demand and constraints on the growth in supplies. The dampening of energy demand as a result of both the sharp rise in energy prices and the onset of the financial and economic crises in 2008 has pushed back the likely onset of an energy crunch, but it has not eliminated the prospect. The countries of the region face the very real prospect that investment in energy supply will not be sufficient to meet future demand.

Supply concerns affect both primary energy supply and derivative supplies (primarily the generation of electricity but also district heating). Developing primary energy resources is becoming more difficult and costly. Oil and gas development opportunities, for example, are moving into harsher and more remote environments. Without substantial discoveries and accelerated investment in infrastructure, oil and gas production will likely plateau over the next 10–20 years. By 2030–35 the region as a whole could move from being a net energy exporter to a net energy importer, unless changes in country energy strategies are made.

Western Europe, heavily dependent on energy imports from the CSE/CIS region, will be affected by declines in primary energy supplies. But it has the financial means to secure the energy it needs.

The CSE/CIS importing countries are caught between Western Europe, with its increasing import needs, and the region's exporters, whose exports to the West will likely decline. They thus face a squeeze—both financially and in their access to energy. A number of these countries have domestic coal resources that can be developed, but growing concerns about greenhouse gas emissions and their impact on climate change will limit how much domestic coal can be used as an alternative to oil and gas imports, especially for countries that are or aspire to become members of the European Union. Other options are to expand nuclear power and renewable energy, and several countries are planning to move aggressively in that direction.

Compounding these difficulties is the deteriorating energy infrastructure, especially for electricity generation and district heating. Electricity generation capacity in the CSE/CIS countries has hardly increased since the early 1990s. Plants are aging, and most thermal plants, especially those that are coal-fired, operate unreliably, use fuel inefficiently, and pollute well above modern standards. The deteriorating capacity has not become a major supply concern only because of the decline in demand during the 1990s.

A number of countries have issued national energy strategies that set out visions for meeting energy needs. But these strategies lack credible indications of how the countries will secure the substantial financing required over the long term. Instead, they tend to rely on general commitments to increasing suppliers' efficiency and developing local renewable supplies to narrow the gap between supply and demand. They do not deal adequately with the tradeoffs among many strategic objectives, such as how to meet international commitments to reduce CO_2 emissions while relying on local hard coal and lignite to supply electricity needs or how to deepen regional cooperation while maintaining sufficient domestic capacity.

The Demand Outlook

Two factors dominate the energy outlook for the countries in the region: the level of energy intensity[1] and the economic outlook. Both are examined here.

Energy Intensity

The level of energy intensity in the CSE/CIS countries was, and remains, substantially higher than that in the countries of the European

FIGURE 2.1

Actual and Projected Energy Intensity in the Russian Federation and Selected Groups of Countries in the Region, 1990–2030

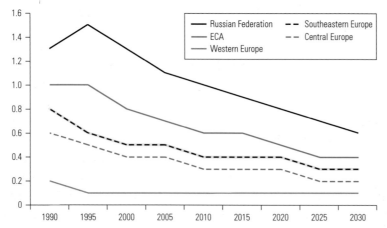

Source: Data for 1990–2005 are from IEA (2008a and 2008b) and World Bank 2007b; data for 2010–30 are World Bank staff projections.

Note: Index is the total primary energy supply (in Ktoe) divided by GDP (in millions of 2004 dollars).

Union: on average the energy intensity in these countries is five times that of the countries of Western Europe. As a consequence, the sharp economic decline that followed the break-up of the Soviet Union was accompanied by a significant reduction in energy consumption, and the economic recovery that began in 1999 was accompanied by an upturn in energy demand.

Energy intensity in these countries, however, has been declining (figure 2.1). For the region as a whole, energy intensity fell from a level of 1.0 in 1990 to 0.7 in 2005. Consequently, while economic growth in the region as a whole had climbed to 10 percent above 1990 levels by 2005, energy levels were still 23 percent below the 1990 levels.

Although the energy intensity gap with the European Union is closing, a gap will remain for some time: it is projected that by 2030, the region's energy intensity will still be three times that of the European Union and the energy intensity of the largest single consumer in the region—the Russian Federation—will be five times that of the European Union. However, Belarus has demonstrated that energy intensity can drop quickly if a government makes the commitment to do so: Belarus decreased its energy intensity by more than 50 percent between 1997 and 2008.

The Economic Outlook

Before the onset of the current economic crisis, the region's economy had been projected to continue to grow at a rate of 5 percent a year (absent any overarching constraints). That would have led to an annual increase of about 3.7 percent in required electricity supply (a 2.4-fold increase by 2030) and a projected increase in primary fuel consumption on the order of 2.2 percent a year (an increase of more than two-thirds over 2007 levels by 2030), with total consumption surpassing 1990 levels in the early 2020s.

The onset of the current crisis has put these growth prospects on hold. The economic decline that affected the region starting in 1990 was such that the region as a whole did not recover to the 1990 level of real output until 2004. As a consequence of globalization, the countries in the region have been particularly hard hit by the current crisis. Focused efforts are being directed at mitigating the impact, with the objective of avoiding another "lost decade." Nonetheless, it remains likely that the region as a whole will recover to the 2008 level of output only by 2013, losing half a decade of economic growth. There are reasonable prospects that, with policy reforms, the region as a whole can resume economic growth at an average rate of almost 5 percent a year after 2011. It is, therefore, expected that the region overall will grow at an average rate of 4.4 percent a year for the 2005–30 period. This compares with the 5.0 percent growth rate projected before the onset of the financial and economic crises.

The assumption of a 4.4 percent growth rate results in a projected annual increase in electricity consumption on the order of 3.1 percent— a 2.1-fold increase by 2030 and an annual increase in primary fuel consumption on the order of 1.9 percent a year (figure 2.2 and table 2.1). Thus, electricity consumption will likely be almost 90 percent above 2007 levels in 2030, and primary fuel consumption will likely be at least 50 percent above 2007 levels.

The assumption of a 4.4 percent GDP growth rate raises the question of the likely impact of a lower GDP growth rate. If GDP were

TABLE 2.1

Average Annual Growth Projections, 2005–30

(*percent*)

Item	Growth rate
GDP	4.4
Electricity consumption	3.1
Primary fuel consumption	1.9

Source: World Bank staff projections.

FIGURE 2.2

Actual and Postcrisis Projected Demand for Electricity in the Region, by Sector, 1990–2030

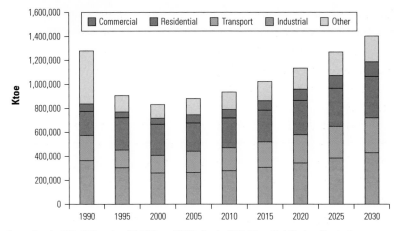

Source: Data for 1990–2055 are from IEA 2008a and 2008b; data for 2010–30 are World Bank staff projections.

1 percent lower (that is, 3.4 percent rather than 4.4 percent), fuel consumption would be about 10 percent below the baseline. The result would be about 0.6 percentage point lower growth in average energy demand.

The Outlook for Primary Energy Supplies

Will the region's primary energy supply be able to keep up with demand projections and still leave a substantial surplus for exports? The answer in the medium term is probably—at least until 2025. But after that the outlook changes dramatically, as production stagnates while consumption catches up.

The region, which produces 15 percent of the world's primary energy, is endowed with about 9 percent of world oil reserves and 31 percent of gas reserves. Substantial resources are concentrated in Russia, Azerbaijan, Kazakhstan, and Turkmenistan. Russia alone accounts for about 10 percent of world primary energy production, 4.5 percent of oil reserves, and 27 percent of gas reserves. Coal resources are more evenly distributed, with Russia, Ukraine, Kazakhstan, Poland, the Czech Republic, Turkey, Serbia, and Kosovo accounting for substantial production and/or reserves.

TABLE 2.2

Gas Reserves and Production, by Country, 2008

Country	Reserves (trillion cubic meters)	Production (billion cubic meters)	Consumption (billion cubic meters)	Reserves-to-production ratio	Reserves-to-consumption ratio
Russian Federation	43.3	601.7	420.2	72	>100
Turkmenistan	7.9	66.1	19.0	>100	>100
Kazakhstan	1.8	30.2	20.6	60	95
Uzbekistan	1.6	62.2	48.7	26	33
Azerbaijan	1.2	14.7	9.3	82	>100
Ukraine	0.9	18.7	59.7	48	15
Romania	0.6	11.5	14.5	52	41

Source: BP 2009.

Gas

During the 1990s, gas production in the region fell to 87 percent of its 1990 level, recovering only by 2005. At the end of 2008, the region had 58 trillion cubic meters of gas reserves (table 2.2). Russia, with the largest proven reserves in the world (43.3 trillion cubic meters), is the world's largest gas exporter. Turkmenistan, Kazakhstan, Uzbekistan, Azerbaijan, Ukraine, and Romania also have sizable reserves of gas.

Russia, Turkmenistan, Kazakhstan, and Azerbaijan, all net gas exporters, have relatively high reserves-to-production and reserves-to-consumption ratios—crude measures of how long they can sustain current production and consumption with existing reserves. Uzbekistan, also an exporter, has lower ratios. Ukraine and Romania are net importers.

Despite concerns about the accuracy of reserve data in some of the countries, the exporters appear to have sufficient proven reserves to maintain current gas production and, potentially, to increase output to meet future demand for both domestic consumption and exports. But to translate those proven reserves into production, these countries will need to make significant investments. This, in turn, will require that they raise substantial capital as well as attract investment and advanced technological know-how into exploration and production.

Russia and Turkmenistan have traditionally been the largest gas exporters in the region. Russia acts as a key supplier of gas to Western Europe and Turkmenistan primarily sends its gas to Russia to meet domestic demand and reexport.

FIGURE 2.3

**Actual and Projected Baseline, Optimistic, and Pessimistic Scenarios
for Natural Gas Production in the Russian Federation, 2005–30**

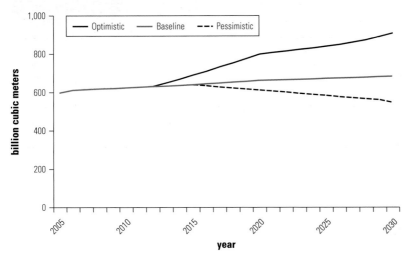

Source: Data for 2005–2007 are from IEA 2008a and 2008b; data for 2008–2030 are World Bank staff projections.

Significant growth in gas production in the region over the next couple of decades will likely have to come primarily from Russia, supplemented by Turkmenistan, unless large fields are discovered elsewhere. Competition by Russia, Europe, and Asia for limited Central Asian gas will continue, with Russia the frontrunner to secure incremental future production.

Russia currently appears able to meet its domestic and export commitments (figure 2.3). If, however, investments continue to stagnate, if no energy efficiency measures are taken in the domestic market, and if Western gas demand continues to rise (a likelihood once the Western European economies recover), Russia may confront supply bottlenecks.

Russia will not run out of gas reserves, but future production and output depend on Gazprom allocating an adequate portion of its cash flow to investment in gas development and state-of-the-art technology, instead of a variety of non-gas-related investments. Insufficient investments in gas development in recent years suggest that Russia has to review its priorities for the sector.

The outlook for production from Turkmenistan is also highly dependent on investment levels; reserves appear to be more than adequate to support increased production levels (figure 2.4). Russia

FIGURE 2.4

Actual and Projected Baseline, Optimistic, and Pessimistic Scenarios for Natural Gas Production in Turkmenistan, 2005–30

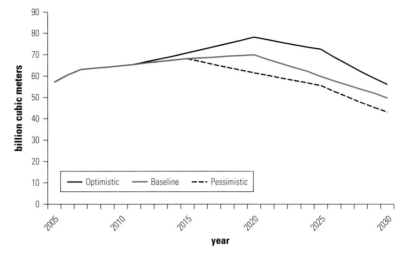

Source: Data for 2005–2007 are from IEA 2008a and 2008b; data for 2008–2030 are World Bank staff projections.

remains the most likely market for the bulk of Turkmenistan's exports, but there is increasing interest in Turkmen gas from both China and Western Europe (via the Caspian Sea, the South Caucasus, and Turkey). There are, however, questions as to when these prospects might materialize.

In the short to medium term, it is unlikely that Kazakhstan will have significant gas available for export (figure 2.5). Most Kazakh gas production (98 percent) is associated gas from oil production, and much of this will be reinjected for reservoir pressure maintenance.

Azerbaijan is expected to increase its natural gas production rapidly over the next several years, thanks to the development of the Shah Deniz field (see figure 2.5). There has also been a substantial increase in the associated gas linked to the Azeri-Chirag-Guneshli oilfields. Oil from those fields is expected to reach peak production in 2010, with a steady supply of oil and associated gas starting to fall off only after 2019. Furthermore, deep gas may exist below the oil reservoir.

Uzbekistan has substantial proven reserves, but its large domestic market will constrain export potential in the short to medium term, without substantial upstream investments and/or drastic energy efficiency measures. Uzbekistan's gas reserves are largely nonassociated gas, most of which supplies the domestic market, with some delivered to Russia, the Kyrgyz Republic, and Tajikistan.

FIGURE 2.5

Actual and Projected Natural Gas Production in Azerbaijan and Kazakhstan, 2005–30

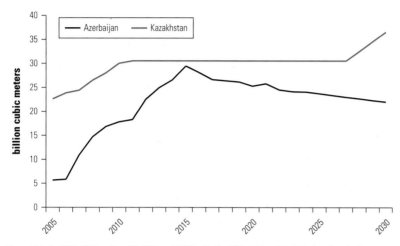

Source: Data for 2005–2007 are from IEA 2008a and 2008b; data for 2008–2030 are World Bank staff projections.

Ukraine is dependent on imports from Russia in addition to its own production in order to meet demand. The underlying reserve base, however, suggests that Ukraine could increase its production levels by about 50 percent if it secures access to state-of-the-art technology, finds partners with the capability to apply that technology, and makes adequate investments.

Oil

During the 1990s, the region's crude oil production fell by almost 40 percent. Starting in 1999 it began to recover, such that in 2008, while the region as a whole was slightly behind its peak production levels of the late 1980s, the countries of the former Soviet Union, with production of 627 million tons, had exceeded their 1987 peak level of 625 million tons (BP 2009).

Oil production and exports have long centered on Russia. During the 1990s, however, both Kazakhstan and Azerbaijan emerged as significant producers and exporters (table 2.3 and figure 2.6).[2] In 2008 these countries produced 605 million tons of oil, or just over 95 percent of the region's total production, equivalent to just over 15 percent of global supply. The three countries have more than 17 billion tons (126 billion barrels) of oil reserves, about 10 percent of global reserves. At 2008 production levels, their reserve-to-production ratio is sufficient for 28 years. These countries will play an important

TABLE 2.3

Oil Reserves, Production, and Consumption in Azerbaijan, Kazakhstan, and the Russian Federation, 2008

(million tons, except where otherwise indicated)

Country	Reserves	Production	Consumption	Reserves-to-production ratio	Reserves-to-consumption ratio
Azerbaijan	1,000	44.7	3.3	22	>100
Kazakhstan	5,300	72.0	10.9	74	>100
Russian Federation	10,800	488.5	130.4	22	83
Total	17,100	605.2	144.6	28	>100

Source: BP 2009.

FIGURE 2.6

Actual and Projected Crude Oil Exports by Azerbaijan, Kazakhstan, and the Russian Federation, 1990–2030

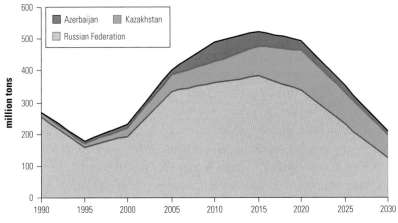

Source: Data for 1990–2008 are from BP 2009; data for 2009–30 are World Bank staff projections.

role as oil producers and exporters, but, absent a major discovery in Azerbaijan and/or Kazakhstan or a change in the outlook for upstream investment in Russia, the most likely scenario is for production to peak in the next several years and to decline after 2020.

Given Russia's proven oil reserves, the baseline scenario projects an increase in production to 500–550 million tons a year by 2010–15, with exports of 350–400 million tons. With the current investment environment in the upstream oil sector, further increases will likely be modest. Production and exports could peak in 2015, with exports falling below 2008 levels by 2018. Because many attractive opportunities to increase production—the "low-hanging fruit"—have already been exploited, it is more difficult and expensive to maintain and expand production.

The outlook for Russian oil production remains uncertain, with serious geological challenges to address. Greenfields in Eastern and Western Siberia could help offset the declining brownfields of Western Siberia, but developing them will require substantial investment, along with the technology to handle the terrain and climate challenges.

Russia's current investment structure appears unlikely to attract the needed investments that would boost production. Over the past few years, the Russian government has steadily increased its stake in the oil sector. The producing assets of two private companies at the forefront of investment—Yukos and Sibneft—are now largely in state hands. The three production sharing agreements (Karyaga, Sakhalin I, and Sakhalin II) were all grandfathered after the 1995 Production Sharing Agreement Law was enacted. There is still a Production Sharing Agreement law and enabling legislation, but there have been no acceptable normative acts and no interest on the part of the Russian authorities in promoting new Production Sharing Agreements. Ownership constraints on foreign investment have dampened the interest of international oil companies in Russia, with restrictive legislation limiting foreign participation in developing new fields.

Two main options exist for offsetting the projected decline in oil production. The first is to promote a more attractive climate for investment in the sector. The second is to modify the tax system, which is heavily oriented toward exports, to make it more inclusive of all production. Applying a consistent progressive tax approach to all production would eliminate a number of economic distortions (including the de facto subsidization of domestic consumption) and increase fiscal revenues over the longer term.

In Azerbaijan the production outlook is dominated by the offshore Azeri-Chirag-Guneshli (ACG) fields, which are expected to operate at 50 million tons a year until 2019.[3] Azerbaijan has opened its oil sector to foreign investment and provided an equitable fiscal regime. However, exploration results over the past decade have been disappointing. The ACG production sharing agreement ends in 2024, giving shareholders of the Azerbaijan International Operating Company a big incentive to maximize recovery before then. The focus for Azerbaijan must thus be on making effective use of its oil revenues to develop the nonoil economy, in anticipation of a time when the country will no longer be resource rich.

Kazakhstan can look forward to a much longer period of high oil production. A steady increase in production is projected until 2020 (even with the delays in the development of major fields such as Kashagan). Production declines, when they come, will be relatively modest, with only a slow drop in production and exports. Even without new discoveries, production is unlikely to drop below 2008 levels before 2030.

Coal

Coal is a big part of the region's energy mix, providing about 23 percent of primary energy supplies and 31 percent of fuel for heat and power generation in 2005. The importance of coal is likely to grow as the region deals with the impending energy crunch.

The region has about 30 percent of the world's recoverable coal reserves (table 2.4).[4] Of that, about 60 percent are in Russia, 15 percent in the Black Sea subregion (primarily in Ukraine), 15 percent in the Caspian and Central Asia subregion (mostly Kazakhstan), 7 percent in Central Europe (mostly Poland), and 3 percent in Southeastern Europe (mostly Serbia). The quality varies across and within subregions, ranging from high-quality thermal and coking coal in Russia to low-quality lignite and brown coal in Southeastern Europe. Mining conditions also vary widely, from lower-cost surface mining in Russia and Central Asia to higher-cost underground mining in Central Europe.

TABLE 2.4

Total Primary Energy and Coal Supplies in the Region, by Country, 2005

Country	Total primary energy supply (Mtoe)	Coal supply (Mtoe)	Coal supply as percentage of primary energy supply	Coal consumption as percentage of total fuel consumption for heat and power	Coal consumption for heat and power as percentage of total coal supply
Russian Federation	647	103	16	22	74
Central Europe	203	85	42	65	71
Poland	93	55	59	94	73
Czech Republic	45	20	45	62	71
Caspian Sea and Central Asia	136	29	21	38	65
Kazakhstan	52	28	53	83	65
Black Sea	264	60	23	20	37
Ukraine	143	37	26	19	34
Turkey	85	22	26	36	43
Southeastern Europe	101	31	30	53	79
Romania	38	9	23	42	68
Bulgaria	20	7	35	47	82
Serbia	17	9	52	79	84
Total	1,351	309	23	31	66

Source: IEA 2008a and 2008b.

Russia, Central Europe, and Central Asia are net exporters of coal. Russia is the most important, accounting for 58 percent of the region's exports and 33 percent of production. Russian coal exports to Western Europe and beyond are limited by the carrying capacity of long-distance railways and Baltic Sea ports. Central Europe accounts for about 30 percent of the region's coal exports, with Poland and the Czech Republic exporting about 20 percent of production to neighboring countries and elsewhere in Europe. Kazakhstan, whose export potential is limited by its location, exports about 20 percent of production to Russia and another 10 percent to other countries. The Black Sea and Southeastern Europe subregions are substantial importers of all fuels, including coal.

Oil is highly tradable. Gas depends on pipeline capacity (except in the case of liquefied natural gas), which places tight logistics constraints on its tradability. It is also expensive to transport—in calorific terms about seven times as expensive as oil. Coal can be transported much more easily; the problem is cost relative to calorific value. The key to the increased usage of coal in the region is its availability: for many countries it is an indigenous resource that is economically attractive, especially in an environment of high oil and gas prices.

Domestic demand will likely determine the future development of coal production. For most countries in the region, domestic demand will likely shift toward coal and away from oil and gas, because coal is cheaper. Its share of heat and power production in the region is likely to rise from 31 percent in 2005 to 37 percent by 2030. For oil- and gas-importing countries, domestic coal also provides better energy security. For exporters such as Russia and Kazakhstan, using domestic coal for heat and power can free more oil and gas for export. The critical challenge is to find ways to make coal use more environmentally acceptable.

Although the reserve base, location of coal basins, and geological and mining conditions are important determinants of supply potential, production will be determined largely by two factors. The first is competition between coal and gas, which is strongly influenced by the price and supply security of gas. The second is the impact of carbon taxes or emission limits, especially for EU countries.

Russia has the geological potential, and the coal industry has the financial potential, to increase production and consumption by 2–4 percent a year. Russia is facing increasing demands on its oil and gas supplies in the domestic market, so coal is likely to become more important, especially if domestic oil and gas demand catches up with supply in the 2020–30 timeframe. Most future coal growth will likely be for power generation in Siberia, to be transmitted to other parts of the country. Although this step would significantly increase carbon emissions, Russia is not constrained by EU limits, although it may choose to limit carbon emissions as a participant in a global agreement on climate change.

In 2005 gas fueled about 57 percent of the country's heat and power generation, coal 22 percent, and nuclear 11 percent (IEA 2008a and 2008b). By 2030 coal's share is expected to increase to 35 percent, which is within the feasible production range. Net exports of coal are expected to increase only if international demand and prices are high enough to warrant a major increase in rail transportation and port capacity. Whatever happens to prices, Russia will remain the main exporter, with modest exports also from Kazakhstan, Poland, and the Czech Republic.

In Central Europe, both Poland and the Czech Republic have sufficient reserves to increase production by up to 2 percent a year, if incremental power and heat generation comes from coal rather than natural gas or other sources. In 2005 electricity for Central Europe came from coal (65 percent), nuclear power (19 percent), and gas (11 percent) (IEA 2008a and 2008b). Future coal development will likely mean expanding production and increasing efficiency at existing mines, although developing new deposits is possible, particularly for coking coal. But production and consumption could also stay at today's levels or even decline, depending on the carbon and other emissions allowances agreed upon with the EU, the cost of purchasing emissions credits, and export prices. Exports of hard coal by Poland and the Czech Republic to inland destinations will likely continue, but the cost structure of the industry means that Poland's exports through Baltic seaports to the rest of Europe may be difficult to keep at current levels in the face of competition from Australia, Russia, and South Africa.

In 2005 in the Caspian and Central Asian subregion, electricity and heat generation was fueled by gas (45 percent), coal (38 percent), and hydropower (8 percent) (IEA 2008a and 2008b). By 2030 it is expected that gas will decline to 41 percent while hydropower will increase to 12 percent. Kazakhstan can expand production through low-cost surface mining. It has the geological and financial potential to increase production and consumption by 2–4 percent a year over 2010–30, making coal the potential principal fuel for heat and power generation.

The Black Sea subregion will remain a coal importer, despite production increases in Ukraine and Turkey. There is potential in this subregion to increase production by 1–3 percent a year over 2010–30 (such an increase assumes that improvements are made in Ukraine and takes into account geological potential and industry and market conditions). Ukraine has a large reserve base to support higher production. The sector has suffered from basic structural, pricing, corruption, financial, economic, ownership, regulatory and institutional issues, but quite a bit of progress has been made with reforms.

Turkey, which is highly dependent on imported gas, looks to lignite and imported coal for supply diversification. It has a much smaller reserve base but a well-functioning lignite sector. Domestic lignite production and coal imports are both likely to increase substantially as alternatives to imported gas—at the cost of higher CO_2 emissions.

A major expansion of coal-fired and nuclear power generation is expected in Turkey and Ukraine. The result is that gas, coal, and nuclear will provide about 30 percent of heat and power in 2030, with the balance coming from other sources, including hydropower.

Southeastern Europe, looking to offset growing dependence on energy imports, is likely to make coal an important avenue for diversification. It has the potential to increase production by 1–3 percent a year over 2010–30, taking into account geological potential and industry and market conditions, although EU emissions targets could constrain member countries. The late 2006 closure of two old nuclear reactors in Bulgaria—once the primary power exporter to Southeastern Europe, supplying up to 60 percent of demand—added considerable stress to the regional power supply. Many Southeastern European countries face shortages and must import electricity from neighbors. In 2005 coal provided 52 percent of heat and power generation, with the remainder split among nuclear (17 percent), gas (14 percent), and other (16 percent) (IEA 2008a and 2008b).

The Overall Outlook

The region's primary energy production is entwined in a web of trade flows, within and outside the region. Almost all of the states and satellite countries of the former Soviet Union depend on Russian gas or infrastructure to meet their gas demand. Many have economies that are highly reliant on gas to meet their energy needs for industry, commerce and homes.

Meanwhile, the region and Western Europe share significant mutual interests with regard to energy supply. The importance of oil and natural gas in Europe's energy mix will make Europe more dependent on imports in the future (table 2.5). According to projections by the IEA (2007a) and the Energy Information Administration (EIA 2007), European production is expected to decline significantly through 2030. Oil production is expected to decline by 50 percent, largely as a result of reductions in North Sea production. Even if oil

TABLE 2.5

Gas Imports by the European Union, 2008

(billion cubic meters)

Item	Quantity imported
Gas piped from Russian Federation	127
Gas piped from Norway	93
Gas piped from Algeria and Libya	45
Liquefied natural gas	50
Total	315

Source: Authors, based on data in BP 2009.

consumption stays flat across the period, Europe's import requirements will increase about 40 percent over 2005 levels. Western
Europe's natural gas production is forecast to decline only 10 percent
by 2030, but strong demand growth had been expected to raise
import requirements more than 120 percent (the current financial
and economic crises may slow demand growth in the near term, but
the trend toward much greater import requirements will remain).
The combination of declining European production and environmental policies favoring less carbon-intensive fuels will significantly
increase Europe's import dependency, especially for natural gas, and
heighten concerns about energy security.

Domestic EU production supplied 38 percent of total gas consumption in 2008. However, the fields of major producers such as the
Netherlands and the United Kingdom will likely decline in the near
future. Rising demand means that EU dependence on gas imports will
likely increase to 65 percent of consumption by 2030.

Russian imports represented just over 25 percent of total supply to
EU countries. Russia will continue to be an important supplier for the
European Union, but it will face competition from other suppliers,
such as Algeria and Norway. In addition, liquefied natural gas is likely
to increase its share in the gas mix above its current 10 percent level.
Other future sources of possible supply include gas from the Caspian
region and Egypt as well as from Iran and Iraq in the longer term,
provided the political situation is conducive to such supply. The
European Union, however, will not be able to find substitutes for a
substantial portion of the gas that Russia supplies.

Russia, supported by other producers from the former Soviet
Union, will continue to be a major energy exporter for at least the
next 10 years. However, looking 20 years ahead, Russia and the other
hydrocarbon producers in the region will not be able to supply Western
Europe with the energy it needs unless there is a significant ramp-up

in new upstream oil and gas investments as well as pipeline investments. The region's total energy surplus for exports almost doubled, from 216 million tons of oil equivalent (Mtoe) in 2000 to 415 Mtoe in 2005. But the rising surplus is expected to peak at about 530 Mtoe in 2015; after 2020 the surplus is projected to decrease rapidly, vanishing by 2030 (figure 2.7). To maintain energy security, Western Europe will need to diversify its future energy supplies to a much larger extent than some may anticipate.

As new fields come on line in Russia and the Caspian Sea, the export surplus of the region's oil and petroleum products is projected to increase steadily, from 297 million tons a year in 2005 to 380 million tons in 2015. By 2020, however, the region's net exports are projected to fall to 327 million tons a year and to turn into a deficit of 15 million tons by 2030, unless the trend of investments in upstream activities changes significantly (figure 2.8).

Net exports of Russian crude oil are expected to increase from 251 million tons a year in 2005 to 310 million in 2015. Production is projected to fall after that, however, with net exports declining to 270 million tons a year by 2020 and to only 77 million by 2030. The region's net exports of petroleum products, at 107 million tons in 2005, are expected to hold steady for longer, but they will fall to 70 million by 2030. The region's net export surplus of crude oil and products is more than able to satisfy Western Europe's oil import

FIGURE 2.7

Actual and Projected Net Energy Exports by Europe and Central Asia, by Type, 1990–2030

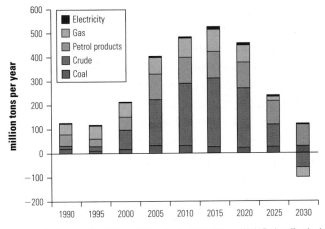

Source: Data for 1990–2005 are from IEA 2008a and 2008b; data for 2010–2030 are World Bank staff projections.

FIGURE 2.8

Actual and Projected Net Oil Exports by Europe and Central Asia, 2005–30

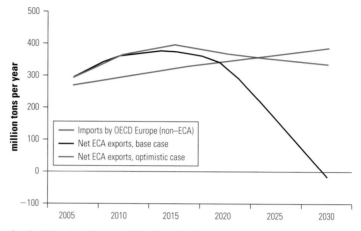

Source: Data for 2005 are from IEA; data for 2010–2030 are World Bank staff projections.

requirements up to 2020. But without major new investments, the surplus will fall rapidly thereafter and vanish by 2030.

If sufficiently large investments are rapidly made in upstream facilities, the outlook could be very different. The EIA, for example, forecasts that the region's oil production will continue to increase, from 593 million tons in 2005 to 941 million tons in 2030 (EIA 2007). In an optimistic case, with the region's oil production assumed to grow at 1.1 percent a year, there could be a net surplus of 370 million tons a year in 2020 and 336 million by 2030.

Net exports of gas are even more important (figure 2.9). Security of supply depends on large long-term investments in transmission pipelines over thousands of miles and in upstream production facilities. Combining the projections for the region's major gas suppliers with an increase in gas demand in the region of 1.75 percent (which takes into account the current economic slowdown), the future for gas supplies from the region to Western Europe—or, alternatively, to China and South Asia—looks bleak.

Sufficient investment in upstream oil and gas structures could moderate much of the disconnect between the region's production capacity and Western Europe's energy needs, at least in the medium term. If sufficient, timely investments are made in upstream production facilities and pipelines, the net export surplus could almost double by 2015, to 137 billion cubic meters, continuing to rise to 182 billion in 2020 before tapering to 143 billion in 2030. The question is whether

FIGURE 2.9

Actual and Projected Net Gas Exports by Europe and Central Asia, 2005–30

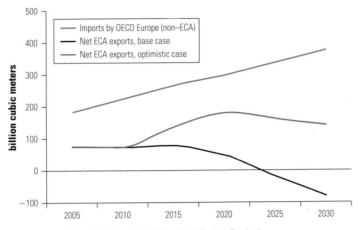

Source: Data for 2005 are from IEA; data for 2010–2030 are World Bank staff projections.

national and corporate policies in the producing countries will foster the necessary investments.

There is a distinct possibility that gas exports from the region will decline, despite expectations in Western Europe that they will rise. Reserves in the region are adequate to meet future demand expectations in Europe, and existing and planned pipeline capacity will be adequate. But investments in gas development are not being made. Gazprom's investments in gas development in recent years have not been enough to maintain production over the longer term, even though investments in upstream activities have been ramped up in recent years. Annual investments on the order of $15 billion are needed to maintain production, and even higher investments are needed to increase it.

Russia can boost supplies, but it will do so only if faced with adequate incentives. Critical among them is assured access to markets. In the past, access has been assured through long-term contracts to EU countries (which Gazprom has always honored). These contracts, however, are expiring, and the European Union seems not to want to replace them with new long-term contracts. This could make it difficult to establish an environment that offers Russia adequate assurance to make the needed investment.

Additional supplies from other producers from the former Soviet Union will be limited over the medium term. The European Union is anxious to diversify its supply sources, but there are questions about gas availability. A number of pipeline projects (such as Nabucco) have been mooted but will not go forward without commitments of gas supply, which have not yet been forthcoming.

Western Europe has the financial means to secure the gas it needs. Asia is rapidly entering the market. Gas-importing countries in the CSE/CIS region, however, may be squeezed as competition drives up prices, and Russia will not feel obliged to guarantee their energy security. New sources of supply are likely to be critical if there is to be increased gasification in Southeastern Europe.

The Outlook for Electricity Supply

The outlook for electricity supply is of even greater concern than the outlook for primary energy supply. The generation plants in the region are old relative to their economic working lives, because investment in capacity has been low since 1990. Nearly 80 percent of all plants were built before 1980. The average age of power plants is 35–40 years. Most thermal plants, especially coal-fired plants, have been operating well beyond the designed working life. Compounding the situation is the lack of major maintenance in the 1990s, a concern that is reemerging in the current financial and economic crises. Many plants operate unreliably, use energy inefficiently, and pollute well above modern standards. As a result, plants in the region can reliably produce much less than their initial rated capacity. The region is now faced with having to confront the effects of decades of neglect.

Electricity generation throughout the region declined nearly 20 percent from 1990 to 1995. By 2005 electricity generation had recovered about half that decline. Thermal power accounted for 66 percent of total generation—half of that from gas, a third from coal, and the rest from petroleum products. Nuclear power accounted for 16 percent, hydropower for 17 percent, and renewable energy for the remaining 1 percent. The countries in the region generated about 2,000 terawatt-hours (TWh) of electricity in 2005,[5] or 11 percent of global generation of 18,195 TWh (IEA 2007a). The region consumed about 1,400 TWh of electricity.[6] Industry accounted for about 47 percent of consumption, followed by the residential (22 percent), and commercial and public services (18 percent) sectors.

The largest share of the region's power generation capacity is in Russia (43 percent), with 22 percent in the Black Sea region, 14 percent in Central Europe, 11 percent in Southeastern Europe, and 9 percent in the Caspian and Central Asia. The region's installed generation capacity was about 500 gigawatts in 2005.

FIGURE 2.10

Changes in Installed Generating Capacity, by Type of Energy and Subregion

a. Increases in Installed Generating Capacity, 1980–2005, by Type of Energy

b. Changes in Installed Generating Capacity, 1995–2000 and 2000–05, by Subregion

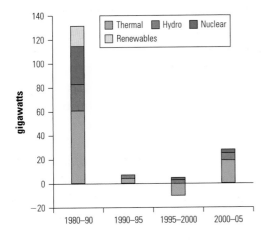

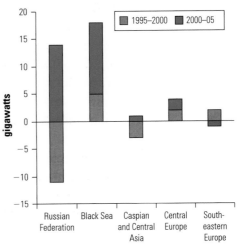

Source: EIA, International Energy Statistics online database.

The region added more than 130 gigawatts to its generating capacity between 1980 and 1990, but only 1.4 gigawatts during the 1990s (figure 2.10). From 2000 to 2005, the region added a small amount of capacity, mostly in Russia and Turkey. The region's share of global capacity declined from 18 percent in 1990 to 13 percent in 2005. Average utilization, however, also fell, from 54 percent in 1980 to 42 percent in 1995 and 2000, as demand declined. By comparison, utilization in industrial countries increased from 45 percent in 1980 to 52 percent in 1995 and 2000.

Private investment was very low: only about $11 billion was invested in the region for new power generation capacity with private participation between 1990 and 2005 (World Bank's Private Participation in Infrastructure database), with a substantial portion (about $7 billion) going to Turkey. Compare with $66 billion in East Asia and the Pacific, $39 billion in Latin America and the Caribbean, and $22 billion in South Asia.[7]

The deterioration in available generating capacity has not yet reached crisis levels for most countries in the region, because falling demand has reduced capacity usage and the current financial and economic crises have stalled demand growth. Even so, electricity importers—including Albania, Bosnia and Herzegovina, Croatia, Kosovo, Montenegro, the former Yugoslav Republic of Macedonia, Slovenia, and Turkey—do face brownouts and blackouts; solutions will be needed to bring supply and demand into balance. The apparent five-year respite resulting from the current financial and economic crises necessitates that commitments for new investments be made immediately, if future disruptions are to be avoided, given the time it takes to prepare and construct new projects.

Even with the current slowdown in demand growth, once the economies in the region start to recover, the anticipated growth in electricity demand is such that the capacity of electricity plants and combined heat and power plants would need to double to satisfy the demand levels projected in the 2030–35 timeframe. These projections, of course, depend on assumptions about both economic growth (discussed earlier) and other factors, including efficiency gains (box 2.1).

Once the economies start to recover electricity generation is expected to increase steadily, reaching 4,300 TWh in the 2030 timeframe—twice the level of 2005 (figure 2.11). Based on national strategies, it is likely that electricity generated from coal and nuclear power will increase about 2.5 times, that from gas will almost double, and

---

BOX 2.1

Assumptions about Efficiency Gains: The Base Case

This report introduces efficiency gains in electricity and heat production in the base case to take into account future technology coming on stream. New and rehabilitated stand-alone power plants and combined heating and power plants will be more efficient than the old stock. The base case assumes that the efficiency of new coal-fired plants will increase gradually, from 35 percent in 2005 and 2009 to 47 percent by 2030, and that the efficiency of new combined cycle gas-fired plants will increase from 50 percent to 59 percent.

For the region as a whole, this assumption increases average efficiency from 34 percent in 2005 to 41 percent in 2030 for coal-fired plants and from 47 percent to 53 percent for gas-fired plants. The effect in the baseline is that 14 percent less coal input and 9 percent less gas input is needed for electricity and heat production by 2030 relative to a scenario with no efficiency gains. Total primary energy demand is 5 percent less, with total fuel consumption unchanged. CO_2 emissions drop 11 percent for coal, 5 percent for gas, and 7 percent in total relative to a scenario with no efficiency gains. The region's energy surplus increases by 64 million tons of oil equivalent.

FIGURE 2.11

Actual and Projected Electricity Production, 2005–30, by Energy Source

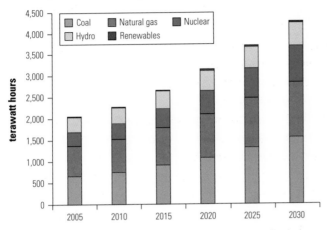

Source: Data for 2005 are from IEA 2008a and 2008b; data for 2010–2030 are World Bank staff projections.

that from hydropower will increase 1.6 times. Generation using other renewable sources, including wind, geothermal, and solar, is expected to grow more rapidly but from a very low base.

The shift in fuel mix toward coal and away from gas reflects two factors. First, hard coal and lignite are much cheaper fuel sources than imported gas, and because of its abundance, coal is subject to less price uncertainty. Second, energy security is an important factor for many countries. Gas production for exports is concentrated in Russia, Azerbaijan, and Turkmenistan. Much of the pipeline capacity (at least to Europe) is controlled by Gazprom. The perception that gas supply has sometimes been used for political leverage has prompted many countries to make a conscious move toward domestically produced coal in their national strategies. Furthermore, the medium-term gas supply picture is uncertain.

Based on these considerations, coal-fired electricity generation is expected to increase from 30 percent of total electricity generation in 2005 to 34 percent in 2030, while gas-fired generation is projected to fall from 34 percent to 30 percent. The problem with this outlook is that CO_2 emissions from coal-fired plants are twice those of gas-fired plants (box 2.2). These national strategies are therefore not sustainable from an environmental point of view.

The expected threefold increase in nuclear power generation over 2005–30 will come partly from new generation in countries with existing facilities (Russia, Ukraine, Romania, Bulgaria). Also likely are a number of new projects that could involve a consortium of countries, as in a new plant to include Poland and Latvia as investors

BOX 2.2

Ominous Implications for CO_2 Emissions

The shift to hard coal and lignite does not bode well for reducing CO_2 emissions without a major shift in generation technology. Using today's technology, the region's CO_2 emissions will surpass 1990 levels by 2015. Emissions will increase by 1.6 times, from 3.3 billion tons in 2005 to 5.3 billion tons in 2030. Even with the slowdown in economic growth, the region's emissions, currently below EU and Kyoto targets of reducing CO_2 emissions to 80 percent of 1990 levels, could break the targets by 2010 in the projections.

Electricity and heat production is by far the biggest culprit. Coal-fired plants emit almost twice as much CO_2 per produced kilowatt-hour as gas-fired plants. With the growing emphasis on coal-fired plants, the share of emissions from electricity and heat plants will increase from 50 percent in 2005 to 53 percent in 2030.

BOX FIGURE

Actual and Projected CO_2 Emissions by Europe and Central Asia, 1990–2030, by Sector

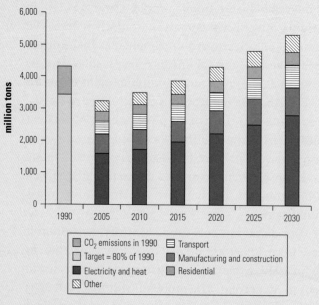

Source: Data for 1990–2005 are from IEA 2007b; data for 2010–30 are World Bank staff projections.

and Lithuania as the host country, as well as single-country investors, such as Turkey. The region has substantial uranium reserves to fuel the new plants concentrated in Kazakhstan, Russia, Uzbekistan, and Ukraine.[8] The share of electricity generation from nuclear power is projected to increase from 16 percent to 20 percent.

In these projections, the share of hydropower is forecast to decrease from 17 percent to 13 percent. Increased use of hydropower would reduce the need for coal, with its associated harmful emissions. However, hydropower has other environmental consequences, and water releases need to be managed so as not to disrupt irrigation needs or create flooding problems. The region's technically exploitable hydropower amounts to a potential 2,646 TWh a year, concentrated in Russia (1,670 TWh), Tajikistan (264 TWh), and Turkey (216 TWh). The region uses only about 13 percent of this potential (World Energy Council 2007).[9]

Efficiency as a Potential Energy Resource

Given the huge costs of producing and delivering energy, the most sustainable kilowatt-hour is the one saved, regardless of how it is produced. But energy efficiency is not free. Energy-efficient technologies have higher investment costs than their less efficient counterparts. Energy consumption constitutes 70–90 percent of the direct life-cycle cost of many such technologies, however, so the cost savings far outweigh the initial investment. And investment in demand-side energy efficiency reduces the need for expensive generation, transmission, and distribution facilities.

Globally, an additional $1 invested in more efficient electrical equipment and appliances could obviate the need for more than $2 in investment on the supply side (IEA 2006c); the ratio could be even higher in non–OECD countries. Energy efficiency should thus be considered as an energy resource on a par with—and even preferred to—supply-side resources. But much potential remains untapped.

Notes

1. Energy intensity is defined as total energy consumed per unit of GDP. At an energy intensity level of 1.0 each 1 percent change in economic growth will be accompanied by a 1 percent change in energy demand. As energy intensity levels reduce the relative energy demand levels also reduce. Thus, at an energy intensity level of 0.5, each percentage change in economic growth will be accompanied by only a 0.5 percentage change in energy demand.
2. Turkmenistan has also been a net exporter of oil outside the region, but the volumes it has exported have not been significant.
3. Announcement by BP Azerbaijan's president Bill Schrader on June 4, 2008 (www.platts.com/Oil/News/8780394.xml).

4. In this report, *coal* refers to the aggregate of anthracite, bituminous coal, brown coal and lignite; *hard coal* refers to the aggregate of anthracite and bituminous coal; and *lignite* refers to the aggregate of brown coal and lignite. Unless otherwise noted, all data are in tons of oil equivalent, for ease of comparison with other energy data.

5. 1 TWh (terawatt-hour) = 1,000 GWh (gigawatt-hour) = 1 million MWh (megawatt-hour) = 1 billion kWh (kilowatt-hour).

6. The difference between total production and consumption includes 320 TWh of power plant consumption, with the balance representing technical and other losses (of about 12.5 percent).

7. The substantial investments for taking ownership or long leases in power companies under divestiture programs do not count as investments that increase generating capacity.

8. The identified resources of uranium at a production cost of $130/kgU are Kazakhstan (816,099 tU), the Russian Federation (172,402 tU), Uzbekistan (155,526 tU), and Ukraine (89,836 tU) (World Energy Council 2007). Identified resources are the sum of recoverable and inferred resources.

9. Technically exploitable hydropower potential is the amount of gross theoretical potential that can be exploited within the limits of current technology.

CHAPTER 3

The Potential
Supply Response

To close the gap between supply and demand, the countries of the region will have to rethink their approach to energy supply. That translates into doing five things:

- Build the capacity for reliable electricity and primary energy supply, and attract the huge investment the region needs to achieve this—$1.8 trillion in primary energy and $1.5 trillion in electricity by 2030—by creating better market conditions and more reasonable tariff regimes.

- Deepen regional cooperation on energy development.

- Reduce the enormous waste on the production side, especially that associated with flared and vented gas.

- Undertake major energy efficiency measures on both the supply and the consumption sides.

- Address potential environmental concerns, and minimize the carbon footprint of the new capacity to be added.

The Primary Energy Supply Response

The potential energy supply response covers both primary energy sources and electricity. The key primary energy sources are gas, oil, coal, nuclear power, and hydropower.

Gas

Developments to support a steady increase in Russian gas production will require capital investment averaging more than $20 billion a year through 2020, with an emphasis on the early years (table 3.1). In addition to the large investment required in exploration and production, domestic gas infrastructure needs to be upgraded, and about 26,000 kilometers of new trunk lines are needed. These requirements highlight the large financial challenges facing Gazprom in the short to medium term. It also calls into question the attractiveness of the Russian gas sector to private investors.

If Gazprom establishes and maintains investment along these lines, Russia's gas production could grow to about 900 billion cubic meters by 2030. But if Gazprom does not invest more aggressively and continues the investment approach of the past several years, production will be much lower, possibly dropping back to 2002 levels (595 billion cubic meters a year) by 2030.

Gazprom needs state-of-the-art technology, particularly for more complex field structures and fields in the harshest environments. One solution is to partner with international oil companies. Partnerships would also offer added funding for capital investments, albeit in exchange for an equity share. Today, however, the business environment is not conducive to investment by major oil companies. The willingness of Gazprom and the government to structure arrangements with adequate incentives—and protection for those incentives—to attract international oil and gas companies will shape the future gas production profile.

The region's wide network of regional gas infrastructure has evolved over the past several decades, mostly to support Russian exports to Europe and trade among the countries of the former Soviet Union. As demand in Western Europe recovers and then continues to grow and new Asian markets emerge for Central Asian gas over the next decade, substantial new gas infrastructure and billions

TABLE 3.1

Estimated Investment Requirements in Russia's Gas Sector, 2010–20
(billions of dollars)

Type of investment	Estimated amount
Geological exploration	26–33
Production costs	44–53
Processing costs	21–22
Transportation (pipelines and so forth)	83–96
Total	173–203

Source: EIA 2005.

of dollars will be required. In addition, Russia will need to invest in a new network to import Central Asian gas to meet increasing domestic and international demand.

Most proposed regional pipelines in the region aim to bring additional gas into the European Union. To reduce dependence on Russia and diversify sources of supply, the European Commission is promoting gas infrastructure to bring in gas from the Caucasus, Central Asia, and the Middle East (for example, the proposed Nabucco pipeline). Gazprom continues to promote regional pipelines in Southeastern, Central, and Northern Europe to secure future access to the lucrative European market with reduced dependence on transit agreements with neighboring countries (for example, the Nord and South Stream projects). Transit countries, particularly undergasified areas in the Western Balkans, may benefit from regional pipelines that help meet their growing demand, if they ever get built (which remains uncertain).

Some proposed pipelines are competing and others are complementary. They are at various stages of development, from early planning (South Stream) to advanced front-end engineering (the Turkey-Greece-Italy pipeline). Not all will go ahead. A key factor will be the still uncertain availability of Caspian and Central Asian gas in the short to medium term.

Two major regional pipelines are in advanced planning, aiming to increase substantially the flow of Central Asian gas to Russia. The two projects will allow Russia to import 90 billion cubic meters a year by 2015 (figure 3.1).

Turkmenistan's gas production capacity needs to be expanded. Gas exports are constrained by the capacity of the Central-Asia-Center pipeline running from Turkmenistan through Uzbekistan and Kazakhstan to Russia, which is currently limited to about 40 billion cubic meters a year. The countries agreed to upgrade capacity to 55 billion cubic meters a year by 2010 and possibly to 90 billion cubic meters a year. In December 2007, Russia, Turkmenistan, and Kazakhstan agreed to construct the Caspian Gas pipeline. With a capacity of up to 20 billion cubic meters a year, the proposed 320-mile pipeline would run parallel to sections of the Central-Asia-Center pipeline to transport gas from Turkmenistan through Kazakhstan to Russia by 2014. It would connect to the Central-Asia-Center pipeline at the Kazakhstan-Russia border. Whether this pipeline will actually be built is still uncertain.

Asian countries, particularly China, are looking to secure gas reserves from Central Asia. Two pipelines—the Turkmenistan-China and the Turkmenistan-Afghanistan-Pakistan pipelines—have been on the planning table for more than 10 years. Their feasibility

FIGURE 3.1

Regional Gas Pipelines Proposed in Southeastern Europe

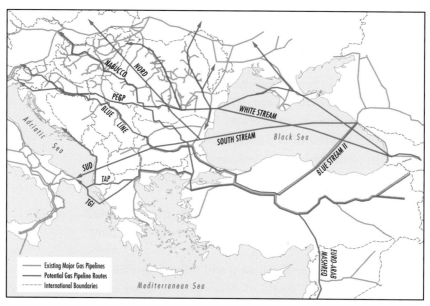

Source: Southeastern Europe Gasification Study 2008.

remains questionable because of the construction costs and the reserve situation in key Central Asian countries, but construction is now proceeding on the Turkmenistan-China pipeline. Thus Russia and China have emerged as the frontrunners to contract the available gas resources from Central Asia.

Oil

For oil, Russia's investment need is mammoth: about $900 billion by 2030, primarily for oilfield technology and infrastructure, according to Fatih Birol, chief economist of the IEA (International Herald Tribune 2006 and Simmons and Murray 2007). The development of new Russian reserves is likely to be one of the most technically challenging and expensive efforts in the history of the industry. Given the scale of future projects in Shtokman, Kovykhta, and other fields in Eastern Siberia and the Arctic, it makes sense for Russia to diversify the risk to more investors. The high indebtedness of Gazprom and Rosneft is also a major concern. In the recent past, these companies have focused on acquiring new assets, not developing existing assets.

Russia's refining sector has considerable private sector involvement. But here, too, investment has lagged. The sector has, however, benefited from the limitations on transportation capacity for exporting crude oil and from distortions in the tax system, which create incentives to refine crude oil and export the products rather than to export the crude. There is also excess capacity in Belarus, following Russia's refusal to continue supplying crude oil at below-market prices.

Managing Oil and Gas Revenue

For oil and gas producers, the uncertainties created by the current economic and financial crises have been compounded by the volatility in oil prices. The sharp run-up in oil prices through mid-2008 generated a significant fiscal windfall. The sense of complacency this created, however, was undermined when oil prices began to drop. Over the medium to longer term, however, oil-related fiscal revenues will remain significant (figure 3.2).

These fiscal projections suggest that the oil-producing countries should have the financial capacity to meet the future investment needs in their energy sectors. However, effective overall management of these fiscal revenue streams must be a priority if these countries are not to succumb to the so-called resource curse.

This means that oil revenue management needs to be effected in combination with the development of sustainable public spending. There are a number of reasons for this. First, there is an intergenerational equity issue. As oil and gas resources are limited in volume, production will be limited in time—spending too much today would entail spending less tomorrow, to the detriment of future generations.

FIGURE 3.2

Actual and Projected Fiscal Revenues from Oil in Azerbaijan, Kazakhstan, and the Russian Federation, 2005–24

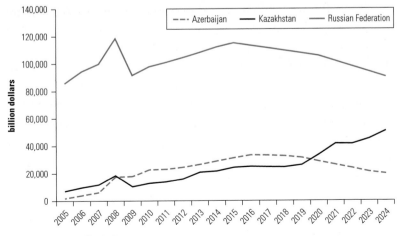

Source: World Bank staff projections.

Note: The assumption underlying the projections is that oil prices will average long-run marginal cost, which is estimated in the range of $60–$70 per barrel in 2008 dollars.

Second, macroeconomic stability must be maintained. Oil price variability may result in cyclical and unpredictable public spending that would increase the real exchange rate and price volatility, which could create uncertainty, adding to investment costs. Moreover, it would lead to upward pressure on the real exchange rate, which would harm the nonoil tradable sector and increase the risk that Dutch disease materializes. Third, smoothing public expenditure maintains spending efficiency.

A viable approach is to follow the permanent income approach, smoothing out spending of oil revenues to a level that can be maintained indefinitely. This is possible by saving in good years and running deficits in bad years, in such a way that accumulated income and investment proceeds provide enough resources to maintain spending levels forever. For macroeconomic management, the capacity to link the consolidated budget—including oil fund expenditures and the medium-term expenditure framework—to long-run fiscal sustainability should be strengthened.

Coal

For coal, the region's investment requirements for 2008–30 are likely to be in the $100–$200 billion range (in 2008 dollars), mainly to add new and sustain existing capacity. Of that, about 50 percent would be required in Russia and Central Asia, where production could grow at 2–4 percent a year; about 40 percent would be required in countries in the Black Sea and Southeastern Europe subregions, where production could grow at about 1–3 percent a year; and about 10 percent would be required in Central Europe, where production could grow by up to 2 percent a year. This level of investment should be well within funding capabilities.

The Electricity Supply Response

Estimates of the generating capacity required to meet the region's projected electricity needs must take into account three key considerations:

- The mix of fuels used to generate the electricity to meet demand, reflecting policies for energy diversity and carbon emissions.

- The substantial portion of today's capacity that should either be retired from service or undergo major rehabilitation to extend its working life or decrease its duty cycle. This capacity is either already in too poor a shape to be counted as reliable or will deteriorate to this condition before 2030 (perhaps sooner if maintenance falls off drastically in the context of the current economic and financial crises). Most generation capacity that was in operation in 2005 will be more than 50 years old in 2030. This consideration applies particularly to the large stock of thermal capacity.

- The expected reduction in the region's power system load factors as its economies shift from heavy industry to light industry and commercial services. This trend reduces the average utilization of the generating capacity that supplies the power system, increasing the installed generation capacity needed to meet demand.

Estimating requirements for future capacity thus starts by compiling the generating capacity in place (using 2005 as a starting point) and then estimating projected capacity retirements, rehabilitations, and additions through 2030. Additions and rehabilitations in the region will increase from nearly 84 gigawatts in 2006–10 to nearly 233 gigawatts in 2026–30 (figure 3.3). Retirement of thermal capacity will accelerate from 23 gigawatts in 2006–10 to 54 gigawatts in 2026–30.

The total investment needed in generation before 2030 amounts to about $970 billion (in 2008 dollars). Thermal generating capacity amounts to about 74 percent of the investment, with 15 percent for nuclear power, 9 percent for hydropower, and 3 percent for renewables. Russia accounts for about 51 percent of the total.

FIGURE 3.3

Projected Capacity Additions, Rehabilitations, and Retirements to the Region's Electricity Infrastructure, 2006–30

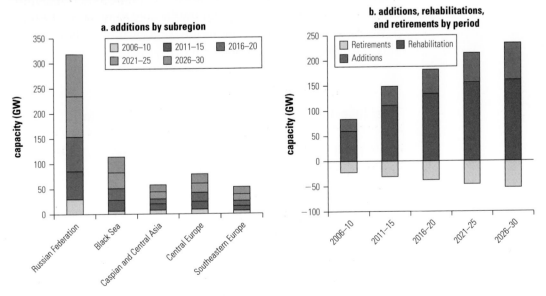

Source: World Bank staff projections.

TABLE 3.2

Projected Investment Needed in Generation, Transmission, and Distribution, by Subregion, 2006–30

(billions of 2008 dollars)

Subregion	2006–10	2011–15	2016–20	2021–25	2026–30	Total
Russian Federation	46	85	106	127	131	494
Black Sea	13	32	42	48	50	184
Caspian and Central Asia	12	20	16	20	21	89
Central Europe	13	22	29	27	30	121
Southeastern Europe	9	14	16	21	22	82
Total generation	93	171	209	243	253	970
Transmission and distribution	50	98	113	131	136	522
Total generation, transmission, and distribution	143	264	322	374	390	1,492

Source: World Bank staff projections.

Note: Investment in generation equals 65 percent of investment in generation, transmission, and distribution.

Upgrading capacity means improving transmission and distribution facilities as well as increasing generation capacity. If investment needs in the region follow the global pattern, generation will account for about 65 percent of total investment in supply; transmission and distribution will account for about 35 percent. These projections imply total supply chain costs out to 2030 of about $1.49 trillion (in 2008 dollars).

The investments shown for the 2006–10 period have not fully materialized; the shortfall will need to be carried over into subsequent periods (table 3.2). Should the countries in the region continue to fall seriously short of the targets, power supply will deteriorate and the countries will not be able to meet their future power needs as reliably, economically, and cleanly as they should. This may affect their future potential GDP growth.

Total Investment Requirements in the Energy Sector

The total projected energy sector investment requirements for the region over the next 20–25 years are huge, amounting to about $3.3 trillion (in 2008 dollars), or some 3 percent of accumulated GDP during that period (table 3.3). This level of investment cannot be provided in this region by the public sector alone. The challenge of attracting private sector investment will require the establishment of an environment that is conducive to such investment. The approach to creating such an environment is discussed later in the report.

TABLE 3.3

Projected Energy Sector Investment Needed in the Region by 2030–35

(billions of 2008 dollars)

Subsector	Amount required
Electricity	1,500
Crude oil	900
Heating	500
Gas	230
Coal	150
Refining	20
Total	3,300

Source: World Bank staff projections.

The Regional Cooperation and Trade Response

Securing investment is not the only requirement to meet future supply needs. Regional cooperation on energy production and transportation is also needed to boost supply security and cut costs. The driving factors are the large mismatches between supply and demand within countries and the uneven concentration of resources, especially the focus on supply in Russia.

Power-trading mechanisms fall into three main categories: bilateral trade between national utilities without competitive procurement, competition in the market for large power users, and full competition in the wholesale market. Bilateral trade applies predominantly to trading between countries in the region. Competition affects trading within some countries in the region but not trade between countries at present.

Many of the region's countries have strong economic incentives to cooperate and trade, because their power markets are too small to exploit substantial economies of scale (examples include nuclear power in Lithuania, lignite-based power in Kosovo, and hydropower in Tajikistan). The region's countries can also trade power advantageously when neighboring power systems have different supply patterns or demand patterns, either daily or seasonally. The ability to trade often takes the form of shared reserve-generation capacity for emergencies. This would be one of the benefits of the European Network of Transmission System Operators for Energy (formerly the Union for the Co-operation of Transmission of Electricity (UCTE), an association of European transmission system operators, for many Central and Eastern European countries.[1] Economic forces also drive cooperation where fuel costs for generating power are lower in one country than an adjoining one, which justifies building power plants to export electricity using the cheaper fuel.

Central Asian countries can exploit the scope for coordinating thermal and hydropower production between summer and winter seasons. Connecting a largely thermal power system with a largely hydropower system allows for energy banking, with the thermal system transmitting energy to the hydropower system during off-peak periods. This energy displaces hydropower in meeting the load on the hydropower system, so water can be stored or banked in the reservoirs. This stored water can then provide power to meet peak demand on the thermal power system.

International trade in electricity falls into two categories. One category is limited trade that influences trading countries' decision about dispatching electricity from their power plants. This trade does not create investment risks, because it uses energy generated from the supply capacity required to meet domestic needs.[2] The other category involves firm commitments to international trade and thus influences decisions about system expansion and investments in new capacity. Committing to international trade offers substantial potential for confronting the region's huge challenges for investing in new capacity. It enables interconnected power systems to work as one larger system, capturing economies of scale with joint planning and implementation for capacity additions and coordinated dispatch of generating plants.

A major issue for deepening electricity trade is covering the risks for investments in new supply capacity and the risks for supply security. Most countries in the region have yet to develop the institutional arrangements to manage these risks. In bilateral trade, the seller/exporter is generally protected through take-or-pay contracts, the purchaser/importer through penalties for failure to deliver or for quality shortfalls. But difficulties in enforcing the contract terms can undermine the intended risk protection. Transnational arrangements and governance reforms for national energy markets are often necessary to mitigate this problem.

Many countries in the region started with opportunistic trade. Some are moving, or plan to move, to deeper trade as they develop their capacity and confidence in the institutional arrangements. Countries such as Bulgaria, Lithuania, Tajikistan, and Ukraine aim to maintain their substantial electricity exports by developing more capacity than needed for their domestic markets. Meanwhile, economies such as Albania, Croatia, Latvia, Kosovo, FYR Macedonia, Montenegro, and the Slovak Republic, recognize their need to import electricity.

Outlined in the appendix are two examples of regional cooperation: southeastern Europe's integrated electricity and gas market under development and projects related to Central Asian regional economic cooperation.

Reducing Energy Waste

The region wastes energy at the point of production, especially through gas flaring and venting. Most flaring occurs when oil production produces associated gas. Gas venting also occurs at gas-processing plants, from pipeline infrastructure, and from other industrial installations.

Some flaring and venting is needed to ensure safe operation. But most associated gas is flared and vented because there is no infrastructure or market to use the gas, so gas is stranded. And because of the relative demand for oil and gas, operators have little incentive to delay oil production to find uses for the associated gas.

In 2006 Russia, Kazakhstan, Azerbaijan Uzbekistan, and Turkmenistan flared 63 billion cubic meters of natural gas, according to a recent survey on gas flaring using satellite data (figure 3.4) (Baugh et al. 2007). This is equivalent to about 1.5 times France's annual consumption of natural gas. The World Bank Global Gas Flaring Reduction (GGFR) public-private partnership estimates that these countries vented 7.8 billion cubic meters of natural gas in 2006.

Russia is the largest gas-flaring nation in the world, flaring and venting 55 billion cubic meters of associated gas in 2006. During the

FIGURE 3.4

Gas Venting and Flaring by the Russian Federation, Kazakhstan, Azerbaijan, Uzbekistan, and Turkmenistan, 2006

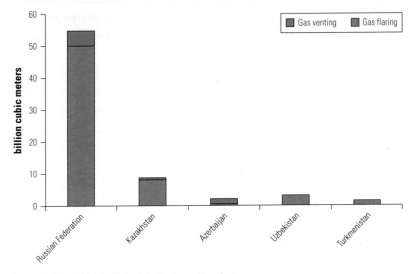

Source: World Bank Global Gas Flaring Reduction Partnership estimates.

same period, Kazakhstan flared and vented 8.8 billion cubic meters, putting it fifth worldwide. Uzbekistan, Turkmenistan, and Azerbaijan flared and vented 7 billion cubic meters of associated gas.

Flaring and venting associated gas wastes potentially valuable energy. At a netback price of natural gas of $150–$300 per thousand cubic meters, the annual value of the region's flared and vented gas is on the order of $10–$20 billion. The region's 70 billion cubic meters a year of flared and vented gas could provide feedstock to 70 gigawatts of combined cycle gas turbine plants (about 2.3 times the installed capacity in Poland).

Flaring and venting also contribute significantly to greenhouse gas emissions. Venting, which releases methane into the atmosphere, contributes eight times as much to global warming as flaring, which burns gas and releases CO_2.[3] In 2006 gas flares in Russia, Kazakhstan, Azerbaijan Uzbekistan, and Turkmenistan contributed 165 million tons of CO_2 equivalents ($MtCO_2e$) into the atmosphere. During the same period, the countries vented 88 $MtCO_2e$, producing 253 $MtCO_2e$ in total emissions.[4]

There are serious challenges to reducing associated gas flaring and venting and promoting its use and commercialization: stranded gas issues, high infrastructure development costs, lack of legal and regulatory incentives for operators to use gas, and the higher value of oil than associated gas. There are no quick fixes, so innovative economic and technical solutions are needed. Best practices around the world show that joint efforts with government and industry commitments can bring substantial flaring and venting reductions in the short to medium term. In 2007 the Global Gas Flaring Reduction study on gas flaring in Russia showed that associated gas is a substantial short-term gas resource that can be developed at relatively low risk and cost—if the government puts in place the necessary regulatory and economic incentives (PCF Energy 2007).

Technical and commercial gas transmission and distribution losses—the difference between the volumes of natural gas supplied to the system and those recorded as consumed—are high in many countries in the region. The lack of meters or the use of faulty meters to measure gas consumption and network requirements are major factors, but substantial volumes of gas are lost through emissions and theft.

The problem is widespread in the region, particularly in the former Soviet Union. In 2005 technical and commercial losses in Uzbekistan accounted for an estimated 18 percent of production (10 billion cubic meters a year). The main culprits: inefficient regulatory systems and a lack of incentives for network owners and operators to adequately maintain and refurbish the gas transmission and distribution network and the associated installations (such as compressors).

Russia's gas transmission and distribution sector is a large emitter of greenhouse gases. In 2006 about 700 billion cubic meters of natural gas flowed through Russia's 153,000 kilometers of high-pressure transmission systems, including imports and transit from Central Asia. Russia also has the world's second-largest distribution system after the United States, with 575,000 kilometers of distribution pipelines, distributing more than 380 billion cubic meters of natural gas to the domestic market each year. About 40 percent (173 billion cubic meters) flows through medium- and low-pressure distribution networks to commercial and residential households.

In 2005 the IEA estimated that 3 percent (or 5.3 billion cubic meters) of the gas distributed through the medium- and low-pressure pipelines in 2004—equivalent to 80 $MtCO_2e$—leaked into the atmosphere (IEA 2006b). Leaks from the transmission pipelines and associated compressors wasted an estimated 6.2 billion cubic meters (93 $MtCO_2e$) in 2004. Total methane emissions from leaks along Russia's transmission and distribution systems were on the order of 12 billion cubic meters (170 $MtCO_2e$) a year in 2004. And more recent estimates put those losses much higher: 10 percent for medium- and low-pressure pipelines and 4–8 percent for high-pressure transit and export pipelines, totaling about 20–25 billion cubic meters a year. Cutting these technical and commercial gas losses will mean preventing gas pipeline corrosion and leaks, upgrading and maintaining pipelines, improving compressor efficiency through rehabilitation and replacement, and installing system metering at all interface points to enable reliable accounting from production to burner-tip consumption.

The countries in the region, particularly Russia, incur substantial gas losses from flaring and pipeline leakages and substantial oil losses from pipeline seepage and refinery emissions. These are both economic losses and environmental harms. To reduce gas flaring and leakages, governments of oil- and gas-exporting countries can provide guidelines and incentives to state-owned and private companies on capturing unused gas that would otherwise be flared, preventing and repairing gas pipeline and oil storage leakages, and reducing gas losses through theft and inadequate or absent metering. They can also open oil and gas pipelines to independent producers, including producers of associated gas from oil.

Notes

1. From an economic perspective, trade across an interconnector should increase until the marginal benefits—from displacing more expensive capacity or from additional sales—equal the marginal cost of transmission across the interconnected network.

2. Some of this supply capacity can be used to generate electricity for export, because it is not fully utilized to meet domestic needs. This type of capacity is used for only short periods of peak domestic loads or held in reserve as cover for unexpected events affecting domestic demand or supply.

3. However, methane's chemical lifetime in the atmosphere is about 12 years. This relatively short atmospheric lifetime makes it a prime target for mitigating global warming over the near future.

4. One billion cubic meters of flared gas produces 2.62 million tons of CO_2 equivalents ($MtCO_2e$). Methane released as a greenhouse gas is 21 times more powerful than CO_2.

CHAPTER 4

The Potential Demand Response: Increasing Energy Efficiency

Investing in energy efficiency achieves three goals, simultaneously and at least cost: lower greenhouse gas emissions, better energy security, and more sustainable economic growth. Energy efficiency is thus a triple-win for governments, end users, market participants (public and private), and society in general.

An additional $1 invested in more-efficient electrical equipment and appliances could avoid more than $2 in supply-side investment. Energy efficiency should therefore be considered as an energy resource, on a par with—and even preferred over—supply-side resources.

But potential remains untapped, because of the many obstacles to investments in energy efficiency. The principal obstacles: inadequate energy prices, lack of payment discipline, insufficient information on suitable technologies, lack of adequate numbers of contractors and service companies, landlord-tenant problems, collateralization issues, and financing constraints.

Governments have a major role to play in promoting energy efficiency. Of course, they must allow energy tariffs to reflect costs. But they must also be proactive in setting and updating energy-efficiency standards for homes, equipment, and vehicles—and enforcing them. Few consumers will take action on energy efficiency on their own—the issue is not significant enough to them. Equipment choices should therefore be limited to those with optimal energy efficiency characteristics.

To set the example, governments should undertake energy efficiency programs in the public sector, disseminating the results through long-term information campaigns. Such a step would stimulate consumer interest and help develop an energy-efficiency industry. Designing cities with alternative means of transport in mind is another important way for governments to raise energy efficiency.

Globally, the technical potential for better energy efficiency through 2030 is greatest in construction (30 percent), followed by industry (21 percent) and transport (17 percent) (IEA 2006a). Reliable projections for the region are not yet available, but given the region's generally poor record on energy efficiency, its potential is believed to be much higher.

Commercial banks are ideal vehicles for financing energy efficiency. But so far the region's banks have shown limited appetite for this line of business. And experience in several OECD countries shows that a dedicated energy efficiency fund is essential as a lender of last resort and originator of bankable projects. Energy service companies are a good solution for large energy consumers (the public sector, industry, pooled residential projects), but they require sophisticated clients and a good legal and contractual framework. There is a broad range of business models for these companies, so countries should assess which have the greatest potential for their market.

Utility demand-side management programs have worked well in some OECD countries in which the regulatory framework provides the proper incentives for utilities. Together with integrated resource planning and electronic markets, utility demand-side management deserves a new look. It is one of the quickest and most effective ways to boost energy efficiency, especially in reaching small consumers with standard solutions—say, through efficient lighting and appliance replacement programs.

The Potential Benefits of Energy Efficiency

Energy efficiency became a major policy issue after the 1973 OPEC oil embargo and the second oil price shock of 1979. The issue was particularly important in Japan and the European Union, both major net importers of energy. Energy efficiency languished during the 1990s, when oil and natural gas prices were low and stable in real terms. Concerns about climate change, energy security, and rising energy prices have again made energy efficiency a worldwide focus.

The terms *energy intensity* and *energy efficiency* are often used together. *Energy intensity* refers to the total energy consumed per unit of GDP, sometimes measured at purchasing power parity prices. *Energy efficiency* refers to the amount of energy derived from a given level of physical output. Higher energy efficiency usually reflects technological or process improvements. Energy efficiency is expressed through a variety of ratios, such as lumens/watt, gigajoules/square meter, and kilometers/liter.

Equating high energy intensity with inefficient use of energy is common but incorrect. Much depends on the structure of the economy, the concentration of the population in climate zones, distances, and other factors. An economy or sector can be both energy efficient and energy intensive if many industries consume a lot of energy.

Although the International Energy Agency (IEA) uses the energy intensity concept to compare energy use across countries and over time, the aggregate indicators can be misleading. For example, Russia's energy intensity dropped significantly between 1999 and 2006 because its GDP grew on average 6.5 percent a year while the share of manufacturing fell from 49 percent to 40 percent. It made little, if any, progress on energy efficiency, however.

Although the 30-year-old market for energy efficiency remains immature, the energy efficiency investments undertaken so far have made a huge difference. The IEA calculates that between 1973 and 1998, energy use in 11 of its member countries grew by 20 percent. These countries would have used 50 percent more energy had they not increased energy efficiency (IEA 2005) (figure 4.1).

FIGURE 4.1

Estimated Effect of Energy Efficiency Improvements on Energy Use in 11 OECD Countries, 1973–97

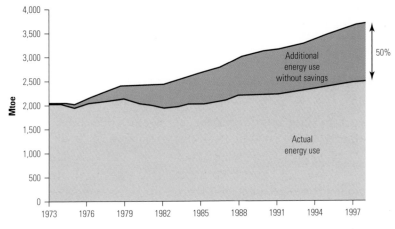

Source: OECD/IEA 2005

The rate of energy savings slowed in the late 1980s, and demand grew much faster after 1990 than before. In the EU15, energy efficiency increased by only 11 percent between 1990 and 2004. Total energy savings were about 100 Mtoe over this period, with individual countries saving 4–20 percent (ADEME 2007).

Because new ways to use electricity are always being invented, energy efficiency is always about playing catch-up. Barring draconian measures to avert catastrophic climate change or huge supply shortages, energy efficiency can only slow the growth of energy consumption.

Given the huge costs of producing and delivering energy, the most sustainable kilowatt-hour is the one saved, regardless of how it is produced. But energy efficiency is not free. Many demand-side, energy-efficient technologies have higher investment costs than their less efficient counterparts. Even so, energy consumption constitutes 70–90 percent of the life-cycle cost of many such technologies, so the energy savings far outweigh the higher initial cost. And investment in demand-side energy efficiency cuts the need for expensive generation, transmission, and distribution facilities.

The explanation for the dominance of supply-side over demand-side options is twofold. On the supply side: a few large utilities with expert professional management, easy access to low-cost credit, a limited number of well-known technologies and contractors, large contracts, and certainty about performance. On the demand side: tens of millions of lay decision makers; hard-to-get and expensive financing; a great variety of technologies, often making unsubstantiated efficiency claims; contractors and service companies of varying quality; small contracts; and projected savings that may not materialize.

Barriers to Energy Efficiency

There are many obstacles to investments in energy efficiency, of which three are key:

- Energy prices often do not internalize all costs, and payment discipline is lacking.
- There is too little information on energy-efficient technologies and too few reliable contractors and service companies.
- Financing is inadequate.

Consumers, manufacturers, and service providers have little incentive to invest in energy efficiency unless energy prices are right. Even more important than absolute prices is that energy expenditures must be a significant share of consumers' disposable income or operating budgets if consumers are to take autonomous action.

In much of the former Soviet Union, average weighted energy prices fall well short of covering costs, and financial cost recovery levels are often artificially low. Price levels in the EU10, Turkey, and the South Caucasus generally cover costs; energy prices in the Western Balkans fall somewhere in between. Countries in the region with relatively low energy prices also tend to have high commercial losses from theft, nonpayment of billed energy, and billing based on norms (for example, surface area of apartment or house) rather than metered consumption. Billing based on norms is particularly prevalent in district heating. About 10–15 percent of the region's electricity, 20–25 percent of its gas, and almost 100 percent of its district heat is sold based on norms. Total losses in the electricity sector can be 50 percent or more of the electricity entering the networks.

In countries with low energy prices and high commercial losses, the prospects for major, sustainable programs for energy efficiency are slim in the short to medium term. With prices of good energy efficiency equipment at world market levels or higher, payback periods would be too long, especially because consumers typically apply high discount rates to these investments (up to 20 percent for households and up to 50 percent for industry) (World Bank 2006; IEA 2007a; McKinsey Global Institute 2007).

But even in countries in which energy prices are low, public sector programs for schools, hospitals, and government buildings can promote comfort and health while generating energy savings. The World Bank's Serbia Energy Efficiency Project—begun in 2004, with additional financing provided in 2007—is an excellent example. Municipal governments have a strong incentive to invest in energy efficiency, because they operate many public facilities and street lighting systems, frequently subsidizing district heating systems and heat consumers. Funding, however, often needs to come from the central government. Energy efficiency may also be a cost-effective part of the safety net for the poor (box 4.1).

Some industries may also have incentives to invest in energy efficiency if they believe that energy prices will rise significantly over the medium to longer term. These incentives will remain weak until energy prices reflect true costs, the real growth path of prices is reasonably certain, and payment discipline prevails.

Too little reliable information and too few qualified service providers are also major barriers to demand-side energy efficiency. It takes a long time to educate consumers; certify energy auditors,

---

BOX 4.1

Subsidizing Energy Efficiency Investments by the Poor in the United Kingdom

Rather than continuing to subsidize the poor's energy consumption, governments would be better off helping the poor reduce their consumption. The U.K. government has 2 million households spending more than 10 percent of their income on energy—the fuel poor. It spent about $4 billion a year on a poorly targeted subsidy.

Energy efficiency investments were the solution. By providing a one-time grant to make homes more energy efficient, the government is saving money, targeting those most in need, reducing waste, creating local job opportunities, improving the environment, and addressing health and social justice issues.

---

manufacturers, and contractors; and introduce and tighten energy building codes and efficiency standards for homes, appliances, and vehicles. Well-designed labeling programs are needed to help consumers make the best choices. In these areas, governments—assisted by nongovernmental organizations and professional associations that have public trust—are best placed to provide this information. The IEA could take the lead in disseminating knowledge—by translating relevant literature into the principal regional languages, for example, and showcasing best practices, so that countries in the region do not have to reinvent the wheel. Funding could come from IEA member countries.

Governments at all levels should undertake energy efficiency programs in the public sector to set the example and disseminate the results via long-term public information campaigns. Such an effort would stimulate consumer interest and the development of an energy efficiency manufacturing industry as well as the necessary ancillary services. Critical steps in bringing about a sound energy efficiency program include formulating an energy efficiency strategy as part of an overall energy strategy; creating an energy efficiency agency (or equivalent institutional focal point) responsible for coordinating at the government level, introducing the necessary legislation, and setting minimum energy efficiency standards; and/or establishing an energy efficiency fund or working through financial intermediaries to provide energy efficiency investment funding. These efforts should be accompanied by a firm commitment—and action—to eliminate relative energy price distortions and to gradually raise energy prices to cost-covering levels, so that all consumers can make rational decisions on the level and type of energy efficiency investments they wish to undertake.

The Potential for More Efficient Energy

Buildings (residential and commercial/public), industry, and transport account for 85 percent of the region's final energy demand: 35 percent for buildings, 30 percent for industry, and 20 percent for transport. Globally, the technical potential for energy savings from improvements in energy efficiency is 30 percent in buildings, 21 percent in industry, and 17 percent in transport. With its old and inefficient assets, the region's potential is believed to be higher (table 4.1).

The easiest time to introduce energy efficiency is when new investments are being made—when a house or industrial plant is built or a new production line introduced. The second best time to do so is when major renovations are needed. The worst time is when there is no other urgent need for renovation or replacement.

The useful lives of assets are key to the speed with which energy efficiency improvements can be introduced. The transport sector (cars and trucks) has the quickest turnover, at about 10–15 years on average, followed by the industrial sector (20 years). Buildings have lives of 50–100 years; they include lighting systems, electrical appliances, and heating and cooling systems that all have much shorter lives.

Governments at all levels have a critical role to play in promoting energy efficiency. Given the abundance of choices in the marketplace and consumers' insufficient knowledge, governments should set minimum efficiency standards and enforce them, introduce labeling, and guard against substandard products poisoning the market, undermining consumer confidence in energy efficiency.

TABLE 4.1

Potential Energy Efficiency Savings in the Russian Federation in 2030

(percent of energy consumption)

Sector	Economic Potential	Financial Potential
Residential	45	25
Industry	41	34
Buildings	37	21
Transport	36	32
Commercial	14	9

Source: World Bank/International Finance Corporation Russia Energy Efficiency team and CENEf.

Note: Economic potential refer to investments which are valuable to the economy as a whole; Financial potential refers to investments which generate attractive returns under current energy prices.

Buildings

In both hot and cold climates, the most critical part of any building for energy efficiency is the envelope—the roof, walls, windows, doors, and insulation. A World Bank project in Cherepovets, Russia that retrofitted 650 buildings during the late 1990s reduced heat demand by 45 percent. Such measures reduce energy use and increase people's comfort, health, and productivity. Linking these benefits can convince consumers to make such investments.

Also important for energy efficiency are space heating, ventilation, and cooling. District heating provides 60 percent of the region's heating and hot water needs, serves about 250 million people, and is an important source of heat and process steam for industry. Its efficiency can be increased, generating significant savings (box 4.3). District cooling uses 80 percent less energy than individual air conditioning systems—an important feature given the expected growth of air conditioning in the region. Electrical heat pumps are now very efficient, reducing energy consumption by more than 50 percent compared with electrical resistance heaters or traditional air conditioning units.

Steps such as those adopted in Central Europe may take 5–10 years to introduce. But the benefits start to accrue quickly when both companies and customers have the incentives and the resources to improve energy efficiency. A key lesson from the comprehensive district heating rehabilitation in Central Europe is that training, information technology systems, and information exchange are vital. Management capacity must also be substantially expanded and financing for modernization mobilized.

Lighting

Lighting is one of the largest end uses of electricity, responsible for 19 percent of demand globally. It accounts for about 13 percent of consumption in the residential sector and 20–60 percent in the commercial

---

BOX 4.2

Very Low-Energy Buildings

Constructing buildings that use very little or no energy on a net basis is technically and economically feasible. "Passive energy" buildings, which use 65–80 percent less energy than traditional buildings, are often cheaper to build than traditional designs. "Zero net energy" buildings are more expensive than traditional designs, but their costs are falling. The European Commission is proposing to make "very low energy" houses the norm for new buildings and to use them as benchmarks in updated building codes.

Source: European Commission 2008b

BOX 4.3

District Heating and Combined Heat and Power Systems: Big Efficiency Gains for the Money

District heating and combined heat and power (CHP) systems—the most efficient ways to use oil, gas, and coal for electricity and heat—are found in many countries in the region. Russia accounts for 72 percent of the region's district heating capacity. The EU10 countries represent another 15 percent; Ukraine, Belarus, and Moldova together account for 7 percent of total capacity.

An estimated 90 percent of the region's district heating and CHP systems need urgent rehabilitation. Modernizing district heating networks on densely built areas, rehabilitating CHP plants, and building new CHP plants would reduce total primary energy consumption by 17 percent, or 860 million tons of oil equivalent, by 2030. It would also reduce greenhouse emissions considerably. The savings would be achieved by putting the waste heat from CHP plants to industrial and municipal use and by reducing thermal losses in the heat distribution chain. The needed investments range from $770 billion for gas CHP to $1 trillion for coal CHP. Of that, $510 billion is needed for heating, the rest for power generation.

Central Europe has made great progress in addressing the problems facing district heating and CHP systems. In Poland, for example, the World Bank undertook a $300 million district heating optimization program in the five largest cities during 1992–99. The program included the following features:

- Control of the district heating systems was automated and changed to on-demand control, giving consumers the ability to regulate heat consumption.

- Investment subsidies were eliminated and household subsidies gradually phased out, from a nationwide average of 78 percent of the heat bill in 1991 to zero in 1998.

- Heating costs fell by 56 percent per square meter in real terms.

- Efficiency gains cut energy use by 22 percent, or 1.2 million tons of coal each year.

End-user measures (substation regulators and meters) could save another 20–25 percent.

Other countries instituting reform face four main challenges: outdated consumer tariffs, split ownership structures, insufficient management capacity, and excessive investment costs. In many countries CHP and district heating users are lobbying against restructuring that would raise tariffs to cover costs.

Lessons from Central Europe suggest that institutional and technological improvements are needed in parallel to stimulate system rehabilitation:

- Heat metering at the substation or building level should become mandatory. Appropriate tariff policies should ensure that both fixed-capacity fees and variable energy use fees are covered, and measures to protect the poor should be put in place. Billing should be based on metered consumption and the related fixed costs.

- From the heat source to building basements, district heating systems should be vertically integrated under a single company, which should be strengthened. Investment, financial planning, marketing, and customer relations functions are all needed.

- Technological renewal, including investment and energy efficiency incentives to foster the change, is a priority. Replacing 10–20 percent of the distribution network can cut thermal losses roughly in half.

BOX 4.4

The Poland Efficient Lighting Project

The $5 million Poland Efficient Lighting Project, funded by the International Finance Corporation and the Global Environmental Facility, transformed Poland's market by subsidizing manufacturers (competitively bid) to reduce the price of compact fluorescent light bulbs from the beginning of the distribution chain. The program dramatically increased the availability and selection of these bulbs, reducing the retail price by 34 percent in real terms. Penetration of the bulbs increased from 11.5 percent of households before the program to 33.2 percent a year after the initiative. The program's direct energy savings were 435.8 GWh.

Source: World Bank and GEF 2006

---

sector. The cost-effective savings potential from energy-efficient lighting is about 40 percent of lighting-related electricity consumption.

Conventional incandescent lights are inefficient: only 5 percent of the input energy is converted into light. The rest turns into heat. Compact fluorescent lights are 4–5 times more efficient and last up to 10 times longer. Newer technologies offer even greater savings (box 4.4). Light-emitting diodes are more than 10 times more efficient than incandescent lights, without the mercury disposal issues of compact fluorescent lights.

Appliances

Appliances—refrigerators, freezers, washers, dryers, dish washers, televisions, and so on—account for more than 30 percent of residential electricity consumption in most countries. They are also one of the fastest-growing energy loads. New technologies can reduce energy consumption by up to 37 percent and offer the lowest lifecycle cost. Standby power accounts for about 10 percent of residential electricity demand. This load can be cut by up to 90 percent, to 1 percent of residential demand. Limiting consumer choice to appliances that meet minimum standards and labeling are key to improving energy efficiency.

By setting standards and transforming markets, the government can relatively painlessly achieve major energy savings in lighting. Electrical and electronic devices are much more expensive, so it is harder to rapidly replace inefficient appliances. Even so, major energy savings are possible. Governments should start by setting and enforcing minimum efficiency standards for appliances and equipment.

Building Codes and Efficiency Standards

Of the highest priority is continually improving building codes and efficiency standards for new buildings and those undergoing major renovation—and enforcing them. Key to doing so is ensuring training for architects and builders in the latest energy-saving techniques. If possible, these codes and standards should be extended to all existing buildings, by far the largest part of the housing stock and the source of the bulk of energy losses. Total energy consumption by existing buildings in the OECD can be reduced by about half over 30 years through renovation (IEA 2008c). This potential savings is bound to be higher in the region because of the generally poor quality of the buildings (box 4.5).

Industry

The region's principal energy-consuming industries are iron and steel, chemicals and petrochemicals, nonferrous metals, and nonmetallic minerals. Together these industries accounted for 62 percent of the industrial sector's total energy consumption in 2005.

Globally, introducing energy efficiency measures in major industrial subsectors can yield energy savings of up to 21 percent by 2030, using proven technologies. In Russia that potential is estimated at

---

BOX 4.5

The Serbia Energy Efficiency Project

The World Bank's Serbia Energy Efficiency Project aims to improve energy efficiency in public buildings in order to generate cost savings and reduce the local and global environmental impact of the use of dirty fuels for heating buildings. The project has two main components: (a) rehabilitation of the heat supply system and energy efficiency improvements in the Clinical Center of Serbia (CCS) and (b) energy efficiency improvements in schools and hospitals across Serbia.

Component 1

The CCS is located in the center of Belgrade. Its heating system consisted of 19 separate boiler plants, some of which were more than 40 years old and 14 of which were fired by lignite and heavy oil. These plants were costly to operate and had very low efficiency and poor reliability. Of particular concern was the pollution caused by burning dirty fuels with old equipment.

This project component included replacing the boilers with a gas-fired cogeneration plant, including extension of a gas pipeline; reconfiguring and modernizing the heat distribution system; and retrofitting the maternity hospital (insulating the roof, replacing the windows, and installing thermostatic regulators). As a result of this investment, heating costs were reduced by about €1.5 million a year. Major reductions in SOx, NOx, ash, and CO_2 were achieved, and the comfort of patients was improved.

(continued)

BOX 4.5

(continued)

Component 2

Energy efficiency improvements for schools and hospitals included roof insulation and repair, wall insulation, door and window replacement, basement ceiling and piping insulation, balancing and thermostatic valves, automatic temperature controls, replacement of boilers and burners, and efficient lighting. Results from the first round are impressive, with reduction in energy consumption of 44–48 percent, together with improvements in the environment and in the comfort of students, teachers, patients, and hospital workers. Schools and hospitals in the program are saving about €70,000 a year on energy, with a payback period of about four years. Some municipalities are now replicating these energy efficiency improvements using their own funds.

The project is financed by a $21 million credit from the International Development Association, approved in 2004. Additional financing of $28 million approved in 2007 is financing similar projects in other hospitals and schools in Serbia.

34 percent, because of the low energy efficiency and frequently outdated technologies of the country's industries (World Bank and IFC 2008).

Savings fall into two categories: sectoral improvements (for example, in the iron and steel sector) and systems or lifecycle improvements (for example, motor systems or recycling). Options for improvement in the two categories overlap and compete with one another, so there is a risk of double counting the gains.

On sectoral improvements, the total potential for energy and feedstock savings is 13–16 percent in chemicals and petrochemicals; 9–18 percent in iron and steel (likely much higher in the countries of the region, because of the prevalence of old and energy-intensive technologies); 6–8 percent in aluminum; 13–25 percent in other non-metallic metals and nonferrous minerals; and 28–33 percent in cement. On systems or lifecycle improvements, the potential gains are an estimated 20–30 percent for motor systems and 10–15 percent for steam systems. Process integration could save an additional 7–15 percent. Recycling metals, synthetics, and natural organic materials and incinerating waste with energy recovery could each bring another 2–4 percent in savings of total industrial energy.

The barriers to investments in industrial energy efficiency are the following:

- Energy costs are often only 3–8 percent of operating costs, so management does not focus on the issue. In addition, operating and investment budgets are typically considered separately.

- Investments are best undertaken when the whole production chain needs an overhaul—something that happens on average only once every 20 years. At other times, the risk of causing a major slowdown is usually considered too great.

- Companies prefer to use investment funds to improve production capacity, often applying very high hurdles to investments. Payback periods of two to five years, equivalent to a discount rate of 20–50 percent, are common because of the rapidly changing economic outlook in many sectors and the need to recoup investments quickly.

Additional barriers are specific to the region. Labor market rigidities force industries to operate intermittently, using fewer than three shifts a day. Real estate market imperfections and high transactions costs force companies and institutions to continue to use buildings that are too large for their needs, leading to wasted energy and inefficiency. Low energy prices and protected domestic industries are also major problems.

Governments can set energy efficiency standards for the buildings and transport sectors—and ensure rigorous enforcement. Doing so is much more difficult in industry, where efficiency decisions are normally best left to plant management, stricter standards may force product lines or plants to close, and an industry may simply relocate to another country depending on the degree of trade liberalization. Even so, governments should push industries to do their part to reduce energy consumption and emissions. Economic incentives, especially positive ones, may be most effective. Energy efficiency measures have been very effective in reducing emissions.

Transport

Transport accounts for about 20 percent of the region's total energy consumption. Almost 60 percent is for road transport, 24 percent for pipeline transport (gas and oil), 9 percent for aviation, and more than 5 percent for railways. The transport sector uses 56 percent of all oil products consumed in the region, 83 percent for the roads subsector.

The transport sector has significant potential for energy efficiency, for two main reasons. First, the vehicle stock turns over relatively rapidly, every 10–15 years on average. Second, the sector is uniquely under the control of national and local governments, which can set and enforce vehicle fuel efficiency standards, promote modal shifts, offer public and other transport options, and improve the design of cities and neighborhoods. The transport sector's market potential for energy efficiency is an estimated 32 percent of consumption in Russia.

The largest savings in vehicle fuel consumption will come through introducing mandatory fuel efficiency standards for cars and trucks—and gradually tightening them. This should start as soon as realistically possible, preferably in all countries in the region, so that manufacturers can plan accordingly and do not need to set up production runs with different fuel economy requirements. Harmonizing fuel efficiency standards would reduce uncertainty and compliance costs for manufacturers and introduce more fuel-efficient vehicles at more affordable prices.

New technologies that improve fuel economy and reduce greenhouse gas emissions will come onto the market through 2030. They include turbo charging, smaller engines, low rolling-resistance tires, low-friction lubricants, idle-stop features, variable valve control, variable compression ratios, advanced air conditioning systems, and new structural design and materials that reduce weight and aerodynamic drag. New diesel engines now achieve 20–40 percent better fuel economy than their gasoline-powered equivalents. Hybrid vehicles consume half the energy today's gasoline vehicles do. Hydrogen fuel cell vehicles may not be a major factor before 2030.

Even with aggressive measures for energy efficiency, however, total energy use in transport will increase sharply through 2030, for two main reasons. First, first-time car ownership is expected to increase across the region, along with a trend toward heavier, more powerful cars. At least initially, many of these cars will also be older second-hand models or inexpensive new models with low fuel efficiency.[1] Second, the declining quality of railways and urban transport will take many years to reverse.

If the experience of the European Union is any indication, the energy use of transport, especially road transport, will increase rapidly before tapering off and eventually declining. Any decline is unlikely before 2030. In the EU15, road traffic increased rapidly between 1970 and 1999, leading to an imbalance among different modes of transportation. Passenger kilometers by car increased almost 150 percent. Bus and coach traffic showed very modest increases, with even more modest increases for railways. For freight, road transport increased by about 215 percent and short-sea shipping by about 150 percent. Rail freight declined by about 15 percent, with no growth in inland waterways.

In addition to introducing and gradually tightening mandatory fuel efficiency standards for cars and trucks, governments in countries in which vehicle fuel prices remain subsidized should consider removing such subsidies. The next best actions would be to increase fuel taxes and to tax high-efficiency fuels less to induce drivers to switch. In the European Union, high fuel taxes have created incentives for consumers and car manufacturers to adopt fuel-efficient technologies, which break even at a lower oil price than in the United States.

Governments should mitigate the trend toward more traffic on roads by encouraging other modes of transport and investing in railways, urban public transport, and shipping, along with the associated infrastructure. Critical for freight traffic will be intermodal shifts (shifting transport from one mode to another); co-modality (using different modes efficiently, on their own and in combination); and interoperability of transport modes between countries. For shifting passenger traffic from cars, the critical issues are integrated ticketing and integrated terminals, where air, rail, bus, and tram come together. Such terminals are especially important given the region's aging population.

Mandatory car labels that clearly indicate fuel consumption and emissions are potentially useful. But most car buyers base their purchase decisions on many other criteria that they consider more important. Labeling and tax incentives—say, tax breaks for efficient fuels and vehicles or tax increases for inefficient fuels and vehicles—could encourage them to buy more efficient vehicles.

Urban planning is critical. Cities, towns, and districts can and should be designed and redesigned to minimize transport needs and with alternative transport in mind (box 4.6). Rather than building the infrastructure to accommodate ever-increasing numbers of cars—which only encourages more cars to come on the road—governments should strive for a reasonable balance early on and invest in alternatives, including walkways and bike paths.

Financing and Managing Energy Efficiency

The three principal mechanisms for financing energy efficiency are financial intermediation, energy service companies, and utility demand-side management. In practice, most markets will need a mix. Utilities and energy service companies need access to funds from the financial sector, and financial sector institutions need energy service companies to aggregate small projects into projects of adequate size. Investment grants and subsidized interest rates are a reasonable trade for

---

BOX 4.6

Eco-Cities

Eco-cities enhance the well-being of citizens and society through integrated urban planning and management that fully harnesses the benefits of ecological systems, and protects and nurtures these assets for future generations. Through their leadership, planning, policies and regulations, institutional measures, strategic collaborations, urban design, and holistic long-term investment strategies, they drastically reduce the net damage to the local and global environment—while simultaneously improving the overall well-being of their citizens and the local economy. They have high-quality public spaces designed for pedestrians and cyclists; high-density housing close to schools and shops; transport systems that favor walking, biking, buses, trams, and trains over cars; and limited private car parking.

A number of innovative best practice cities around the world have demonstrated how ecological and economic progress can go hand-in-hand. For example;

- Stockholm in Sweden has demonstrated how integrated and collaborative planning and management can transform an old inner city industrial area into an attractive and ecologically sustainable district based on a cyclical urban metabolism. The district is seamlessly integrated into the larger urban fabric, and has provided inspiration for more initiatives in the city and catalyzed change. Some of the initial results have been a 30% reduction in non-renewable energy use and a 41% reduction in water use.

- Curitiba in Brazil has implemented innovative approaches in urban planning, city management and transport planning. The city has been able to sustainably absorb a population increase from 361,000 (in 1960) to 1,797,000 (in 2007). Most well known for its innovative Bus Rapid Transit system, Curitiba has found innovative solutions to practically every dimension of planning—and most importantly created an enduring culture of sustainability.

- Yokohama, Japan's second largest city, has demonstrated how an integrated approach to waste management, combined with stakeholder engagement, could reduce solid waste by 38.7% during a period when population actually grew by 170,000. This significant waste reduction allowed Yokohama to save US$1.1 billion, which was otherwise required for the renewal of two incinerators, as well as US$ 6 million annual operation and maintenance costs.

Several EU countries have built eco-cities, eco-towns, and eco-districts, and momentum is growing, with Sweden and the United Kingdom planning a significant number over the next decade. China is also planning to create an eco-city.

Source: World Bank 2009

any programmatic carbon credits the government receives from energy efficiency investments in the residential sector. Specialization and standardization of the products offered are key for market actors in all three categories.

Commercial Banks

The financial services sector should be the place consumers go when they need financing for energy efficiency investments. This has not yet happened, because commercial banks in many transition economies were extremely risk averse in the 1990s. Before the financial crisis hit, banks were branching into new areas of lending, partly in response to competitive pressures from foreign banks and partly as a result of local banks' increased exposure to their customers. For the time being, however, this process has stalled. The International Finance Corporation believes that banks can move from "defensive banking," in which environmental management is only a risk and a cost, to "sustainable banking," in which sustainable development is an opportunity for growth (IFC 2007). This shift builds customer loyalty, protects market share, helps banks differentiate themselves from competitors, and improves their brand. However, it may not materialize until after financial and economic recovery is well underway in the region.

Experience with international financial institutions' credit lines to banks has been unsatisfactory, for several reasons. First, a commercial approach has been lacking, along with the incentives for banks to market credit lines. Second, banks have not addressed such key barriers as weak capacity for project development and high perceived project risks and transactions costs.

Despite these failures, there is growing consensus that commercial banks are, in principle, the best vehicle for sustainably financing energy efficiency. Because commercial banks are already important in financing homes, factories, cars, and other energy-consuming assets, they could become a prime conduit for consumer incentives to buy assets that exceed regulations and norms for energy efficiency. Banks could provide credit to enable customers to purchase assets to reduce their energy consumption. When it comes to energy efficiency, however, most banks lack the expertise to evaluate investments: the market currently appears small, repayments are based not on revenues but on projected (and uncertain) energy savings, and collateral is usually not liquid or portable. Residential energy efficiency projects are often small, so transaction costs are high; banks prefer larger, more creditworthy customers and projects for lending or leasing. For banks to have confidence in forecasts of energy savings, energy auditors need to be certified and measurements standardized.

Credit lines from international financial institutions in several Central and Southeastern European countries currently fund partial guarantee programs and technical assistance to help banks build capacity for risk assessment and developing deal flow.[2] There is not yet enough experience to indicate if the new approach will bring sustainable, long-term lending for energy efficiency—or if the banks will revert to other lending once the technical assistance stops, guarantee programs phase out, and investment grant funds cease to flow. An independent review of the experience so far is needed.

Banks that see energy efficiency as a long-term opportunity should specialize in particular areas and products, making it easier for them to assess project risks and establish a brand. The objective should be to make the transaction for both parties as easy as, say, making and obtaining a car loan.

Energy Efficiency Funds

Dedicated revolving energy efficiency funds are indispensable in countries in which investing in energy efficiency is in its early stages and the banking sector is not ready to provide financing (box 4.7). Well-capitalized funds dedicated to energy efficiency may be the only way to establish adequate funding channels in such cases. These funds can kick-start an energy efficiency market by developing a solid project pipeline, among other benefits. They can also build a critical mass of loan and project performance data that banks can later use— on a fee-for-service basis—to better assess and price risks.

Energy efficiency funds are in principle transitional, so an exit strategy should be in place, to be implemented if and when the banking sector is ready to permanently take over the role of the funds. But countries should guard against prematurely phasing out the funds: experience in several IEA/EU countries with sophisticated banking

---

BOX 4.7

The Bulgarian Energy Efficiency Fund

The Global Environmental Facility and the World Bank approved a $10 million grant in 2005 to provide the bulk of initial capitalization for the Bulgarian Energy Efficiency Fund (BEEF), a revolving fund. The seed capital of $16 million included contributions from the Bulgarian and Austrian governments and private Bulgarian firms. The fund is characterized by a flexible combination of financial products, public-private partnership in its capitalization and management, strong country ownership, a manager with strong financial skills and local knowledge, and a solid pipeline of finance-ready projects. Because the BEEF has already funded 42 projects, its capitalization should soon rise.

Source: Energy Charter Secretariat 2008.

sectors shows that commercial banks remain hesitant about energy efficiency lending and that investors and financiers remain reluctant to invest in energy efficiency.[3] Reducing the financing barrier is thus a long-term task. For that reason, maintaining a well-capitalized energy efficiency fund as a lender of last resort is desirable, especially in countries in which the commercial case for energy efficiency investments remains weak.

Energy Service Companies

An energy service company (ESCO) implements projects to improve energy efficiency in a consumer's facility. The purest form is energy performance contracting, under which the energy service company guarantees equipment performance and uses the resulting energy savings to fund the investment and its own services. The energy service company typically arranges the financing package, but the actual financing could come from a commercial bank, the service company, or the consumer.

The full-service business model offers technical and financial support for preparing, financing, and implementing energy efficiency projects. But energy service companies have not found ready acceptance. The contracts are complex; prospective clients are skeptical about the promised energy savings, which are monitored by the very company that promises them; and financing is not always readily available. Even so, energy service companies remain a good solution for large energy consumers (say, the public sector and industry) that have some expertise in energy and can access support on the legal and contractual issues that arise in dealing with energy service companies.

The public buildings sector is a core market in which the model has been successful in the European Union and the United States, mostly in retrofitting large buildings for energy efficiency. Ownership and tenancy of the facilities is often clear, the risk of bankruptcy limited, and the risk of closure low. But obstacles remain. Some facilities may have been leased from private owners, splitting incentives for energy efficiency. Public authorities also have little incentive to reduce energy costs if they cannot use the savings for other purposes. There is often less competence in the public sector than in industry in managing energy use and addressing the commercial and financial complexity of energy performance contracting. In many countries in the region, forgoing savings is often seen as preferable to "giving away savings" to a private company. And public procurement policies need adaptation to enable 5- to 10-year turnkey contracting with a service company, with bid valuation based on results rather than just the lowest price.

In industry, energy demand depends on many factors, including the production process and product mix. Measuring energy efficiency gains from a particular investment can thus be difficult. For energy performance contracting to succeed, an industry must meet several conditions, such as the following:

- Its economic outlook is sound.
- It has experience with outsourcing services.
- Few staff are responsible for the energy system.
- It has an obvious energy problem in urgent need of a solution.
- The parts of the energy system that need to be improved can be clearly identified and are not critical for production.
- The production process is not overly complex or confidential.
- The energy supply and use chain can be separated into different elements.
- Energy costs are of medium or high importance in overall costs, with a clear impact on profits.

Energy service companies are interested in the residential sector only if many individual projects can be aggregated. Because of high transactions costs, a project of about $150,000 is often considered the minimum for viable energy performance contracting. Germany, where public housing projects are typically bundled in pools of about 100 separate projects, offers a good example of the critical mass needed. Under all scenarios, service companies need access to readily available funding from local banks—something that is hard to obtain in a number of countries in the region.

Among the EU10+2, Hungary has the most successful energy services industry. Making an early start in the 1980s—laying the foundations for legal, institutional, and technical expertise—was critical, as were energy-sector restructuring, good institutional and banking reforms, and structured aid programs. Utility energy service companies are developing rapidly and increasing their market share. In Hungary electric utilities have territorial monopolies for supplying electricity, not for other services. As in Denmark and the United Kingdom, one way to expand into the territory of another utility is by doing energy services projects.[4]

There are many business models for energy service companies (box 4.8). All ultimately lead to energy savings. The full-service model is attractive, but lack of proper legal and financial infrastructure, and local companies' limited ability to raise capital and to take on and manage risks, can make this model nonviable in the short

---

BOX 4.8

A Utility Energy Service Company in Croatia

HEP Energy Service Company, part of Croatia's national electricity utility, was created in 2003, with support from a World Bank loan and a Global Environmental Facility grant (World Bank 2003). Sales surpassed $10 million a year in 2008, showing the potential of utility-based energy service companies. While building the business, the company benefited from its affiliation with HEP, Croatia's national electricity company, through name recognition, access to HEP's consumer database, and initial financial support from the parent company, which facilitated taking a long-term perspective. HEP Energy Service Company has a good sales strategy and dedicated internal sales and marketing. The fact that it works on all energy applications has increased its potential market.

Source: World Bank 2003

---

and medium term. Countries should test a variety of models and determine which have the most potential for their markets.

The technical, legal, and financial infrastructure to support the full-service business model is still absent in many countries in the region. On technical capabilities, energy audits and monitoring and verification of savings are particularly important. On the legal framework, all parties need confidence that contracts are enforceable. Financially, the banking sector must be willing to help finance energy performance contracting, an unfamiliar product for most institutions. Governments can help develop an energy services industry and the supporting infrastructure with public sector investments in energy efficiency. Specializing in a few standardized products would help energy service companies build credibility among consumers and banks, which would enable them to expand.

Utility Demand-Side Management

Under demand-side management programs, energy utilities (usually distribution companies) organize all aspects of energy-efficient delivery—financing through ratepayer-funded programs, technical development, and interface with consumers. Demand-side management programs include curtailing or shifting loads during peak periods (load management) and increasing end users' energy efficiency, often by disseminating information and offering discounts for energy-efficient lighting and appliances.

The original goal of most demand management programs was to postpone the need for new power sources, including generating facilities, power purchases, and transmission and distribution capacity. This goal persists, but three other goals have become important as well, namely, gaining customers' loyalty by helping them control their bills; cultivating a "green" image; and improving collections, reducing losses, and connecting more consumers.

Utility demand-side management can be a good model because combining energy delivery and energy efficiency can allow a utility to provide services at the lowest cost. The utility has detailed knowledge of its consumers, including energy consumption data, in-house metering and data gathering for impact evaluation, personal records and payment history, and an organized system for monthly billing and collection.

Despite these advantages, the experience of utility demand-side management has been mixed, for three reasons. First, utilities are often regulated based on price caps, meaning that revenues depend on the volume of electricity sold. Second, demand-side management can provide real resources quickly and cheaply, but its value is often discounted, because it is seen as less tangible and thus less reliable than traditional supply-side investments. Third, demand-side management is often seen as a distraction from the real utility business—and not good for one's career. These biases can change.

The simplest way to cut the link between revenues and electricity sales is to regulate revenues, not prices. An alternative is a hybrid approach that maintains price caps but mandates demand-side management (as in California, Denmark, and the United Kingdom). The European Union's white certificate system takes a similar approach. The core principle is to impose efficiency targets on energy suppliers but to leave the market free to choose the best solution.

For planning, a regulator can require that utilities consider demand-side management on a par with supply options for generation and network planning, or even as the first resource in the loading order. But such integrated resource planning requires significant institutional capacity for the regulator. One option is market testing: the utility calls for expressions of interest for lower demand; the market, not the utility, then evaluates demand-side management options and takes on the commercial risk. In many countries, the Internet now makes possible market testing in real-time electronic markets. This approach also levels the playing field between the demand side and the supply side in bidding for "negative capacity."

Eliminating the regulatory and planning biases is a good start. But the cultural bias should not be underestimated. To change mindsets, utility general managers must champion demand-side management and appoint a rising star to head the group, which should receive at least as much resources and staffing as the rest of the utility.

As restructuring unbundles the energy sector into generation, transmission, distribution, and supply, planning and contracting for demand-side management become more complex. A demand management program may be of value to all four links in the energy supply chain, so unbundling more effectively reveals the value of demand-side management for different parties. The result is a trend toward more network-driven, rather than just capacity-driven, demand-side management.

Utility demand-side management and integrated resource planning using electronic markets thus deserve a new look by governments. Regulators should be pushed much harder to adopt these quick and effective ways to boost energy efficiency. By ensuring broad-based implementation, these programs can be especially effective in reaching small consumers with standard solutions—say, through efficient lighting and appliance replacement programs. To succeed, such efforts require a competent regulator and a regulatory framework that gives utilities the proper incentives, good metering, and consumer confidence in both the utility and its energy efficiency contractors. These conditions do not yet exist in all countries in the region, but more are approaching readiness. Turkey and most EU10+2 countries are prime candidates.

The Need for a Comprehensive Action Plan

Energy efficiency is a triple-win for governments, end users, market participants (public and private), and society in general. But energy efficiency measures are not going to be implemented without changes in the incentive framework. Lessons from Belarus, Denmark, and Sweden show that significant progress can be achieved in a relatively short time if governments play a proactive and steadfast role; develop the legal and institutional basis; allow energy tariffs to reflect costs; foster financing mechanisms and provide economic incentives; set and enforce energy-efficiency codes and standards for homes, equipment, and vehicles; and spearhead the energy efficiency agenda within the public sector itself and with society at large (box 4.9).

BOX 4.9

An Energy Efficiency Checklist for Governments

A. Legislation and strategy
Energy law
Energy efficiency law
Energy strategy
Energy efficiency strategy
Law on homeowners' associations
Other enabling legislation

B. Institutional
Energy efficiency agency
Independent energy regulatory agency

C. Energy prices
Relative energy prices right
Absolute energy prices that reflect costs

D. Financing mechanisms
Energy efficiency fund
Commercial bank lending
Utility demand-side management
Energy services companies

E. Public sector as champion
Public buildings program
Energy poverty reduction program
Information campaigns
National spatial plan with a focus on energy
    efficiency
Urban development plans with a focus on
    energy efficiency

F. Codes and standards
Buildings
    Building codes
    Effective enforcement (for example, usage
        licenses)
    Appliance standards
    Lighting standards
Industry
    Voluntary agreements
    Mandatory cogeneration potential review
Transport
    Vehicle fuel efficiency standards
    Periodic vehicle inspections
    Fuel taxes
Labels
    Cars
    Appliances
    Homes

G. Economic incentives
Tax reductions
Vehicle fuel taxes
Interest rate subsidies
Investment grants
Tradable permits

H. Civic
Professional organizations
Environmental nongovernmental organizations
"Soft infrastructure" (energy efficiency
    brainpower)

Notes

1. Russian-made VAZ and GAZ passenger cars, for example, have fuel consumption that is 50 percent higher than that of equivalent cars produced in the OECD; the fuel consumption of Kamaz trucks is 100 percent higher. Protection of the Russian car industry results in an additional 7–8 Mtoe of fuel consumption annually, or 23–38 percent of total demand (Aslanyan 2006).

2. In Bulgaria, the European Bank for Reconstruction and Development is providing investment grants of up to 20 percent to consumers, and incentive payments to the banks, from the Kozloduy nuclear power plant decommissioning support fund.

3. In its recommendations to the G8 2007 Summit, the IEA called for governments to establish public-private tools to facilitate energy efficiency funding. In Spain, for example, revolving energy efficiency funds still offer 80–100 percent financing for qualifying projects.

4. Utility energy service companies may be a good compromise solution between pure utility demand-side management and nonutility energy service companies. They have many of the advantages of utility demand-side management and are not subject to regulatory restrictions on income, which guarantees the financial incentive for the utility.

CHAPTER 5

The Environmental Conundrum

Concerns about supply security have caused many countries in the region to start looking at domestic energy resources and diversification options with only minimal consideration of the environmental consequences. This has created an environmental conundrum. The challenge for these countries going forward will be to secure additional energy supplies quickly and at minimum cost while under pressure to act in an environmentally friendly fashion and limit the growth of greenhouse gas emissions.

The international consensus is that global climate change was accelerating rapidly before the onset of the financial and economic crises. Although the growth in emissions has slowed for the time being, concerns remain that the impact could be severe, even with drastic measures to abate emissions. The region's carbon emissions fell during the 1990s, but they rose with economic recovery. Although the current economic crisis may provide some respite emissions will again rise as economies recover.

Relative to GDP, carbon emissions in the region are among the highest in the world. In 2005 Russia was the third largest CO_2 emitter in the world, after the United States and China. Despite their reliance on domestic coal, the region's EU members have already started tackling climate change, improving energy efficiency, developing renewable energy technologies, and tapping carbon finance.

Other countries in the region need to catch up on the agenda—and quickly.

The Kyoto Protocol and trading under the European Union's emission trading scheme of 2005 are major steps forward, providing opportunities for low-cost mitigation of carbon emissions. The 2006 Stern Review (2006) on the economics of climate change, the Intergovernmental Panel on Climate Change's *Fourth Assessment Report* (IPCC 2007), and the 2007 UN Conference of Parties in Bali have sustained the momentum and created an international platform to address climate change.

The European Union is taking the lead, with clear targets for greenhouse gas reductions and policies to achieve them. The core objective of the Energy Policy for Europe is a 20 percent reduction in greenhouse gas emissions by 2020 against 1990 levels (Commission of the European Communities 2007). For energy efficiency, the target is a 20 percent improvement by 2020. For renewable energy, the target is an energy mix with 20 percent renewables by 2020. These targets are aggressive, requiring stringent measures by individual members.

There is a disconnect between global efforts to reduce carbon emissions and the region's national energy strategies for the next 20 years. The region's policymakers and businesses must rethink these strategies and engage seriously in global efforts. Demands for carbon reduction will only intensify; the region must do its share. But transitioning to a low-carbon economy can be costly, depending on the target. By tapping into carbon finance, the region can reduce its carbon footprint and attract critical capital to rebuild its energy infrastructure and industrial base using efficient and cleaner technologies.

The Kyoto Protocol and the development of the carbon trading market have created instruments with which to leverage investments in greenhouse gas reductions: project-based arrangements, the cap-and-trade EU energy trading scheme, international emissions trading, and the trading of assigned amount units (rights to emit) all prove to be big opportunities for countries in the region. Governments should ensure that national policies and legislation facilitate these instruments, foster rapid technological modernization, and form a revolution toward energy efficiency. In addition, carbon taxes and standards setting can create incentives for corporations and consumers to change.

The CIS/CSE region is the only region in which CO_2 emissions have declined since 1990. In the prior decade, emissions grew at 4.8 percent a year. After the economic contraction of the 1990s, emissions declined 38.7 percent, from 5.2 billion metric tons in 1988 to 3.3 billion in 2005 (17 percent of the global total) (World Bank

2008c). But fuel consumption and emissions started to rise again once economies began to recover. Although this rise has been stalled by the 2008/09 economic and financial crises, once the region's rapid economic growth resumes, that growth, coupled with high energy intensity and low energy efficiency, will result in renewed growth of emissions.

In 2005 the region's largest emitters of CO_2 were Russia (1.5 billion tons), Ukraine (305 million tons), Poland (296 million tons), Turkey (209 million tons), Kazakhstan (162 million tons), and Uzbekistan (126 million tons) (figure 5.1). These high emission rates reflect the region's reliance on abundant domestic coal, low energy efficiency, and outdated technology.

Per capita emissions vary across the region, averaging 5.5 metric tons of CO_2 per capita per year in 2005 (by way of comparison, average per capita emissions were 20.2 tons in the United States and 4.2 tons in China). At 11.8 tons of carbon, Russia's per capita emissions in 2005 were the third-highest in the region, behind the Czech Republic and Estonia.[1] Poland's CO_2 emissions per capita were 8.5 tons a year. Other countries in the region with high per capita emissions are Kazakhstan, Turkmenistan, and Ukraine.

FIGURE 5.1

Total CO_2 Emissions in the Region, by Country, 2005

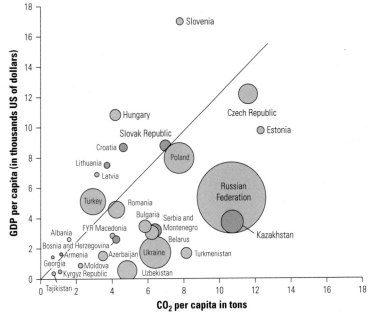

Source: World Bank 2007b and IEA 2007b.

Note: The size of the bubble indicates the magnitude of total CO_2 emissions.

FIGURE 5.2

Carbon Intensities in CSE/CIS Subregions and Other Countries, 2005

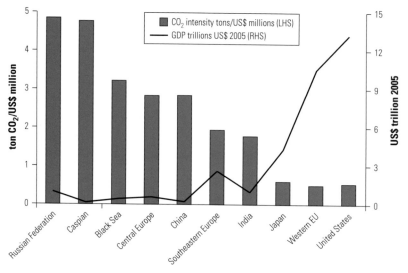

Source: IEA 2005.

Figure 5.1 shows the variations in CO_2 emissions by GDP per capita. Countries to the left of the 45 degree line, such as Hungary and Turkey, have relatively low emissions, given their level of GDP.

CO_2 intensity is a rough measure of a country's potential for switching fuels—replacing high-carbon fuels (for example, coal) with low-carbon fuels (for example, gas or renewable energy). Carbon intensity in the region is much higher than in most other regions (figure 5.2).

Emissions by CSE/CIS countries in 2005 were at 69 percent of their 1990 levels—below the targets of the Kyoto Protocol and the European Union. The baseline projections in this report are based on current technology in terms of carbon emission per ton of fuel input for various output categories according to the IEA. No carbon capture and sequestration technologies are applied.

The region's heavy reliance on coal, low energy efficiency, and high energy intensity will lead to sustained increases of CO_2 emissions in the baseline scenario. Total CO_2 emissions will likely increase from 3.3 billion tons in 2005 to about 3.9 billion tons in 2015 and 5.3 billion tons in 2030 (figure 5.3). Under this "business as usual" scenario, the region will breach the 20 percent reduction target of the European Union by 2010, reaching 1990 levels by 2020. The shift to coal- and lignite-fired power plants will exacerbate the rapid rise. The share of emissions from these electricity and heat plants will increase to two-thirds of all emissions.

FIGURE 5.3

Actual and Projected CO$_2$ Emissions in the Region, 1990–2030

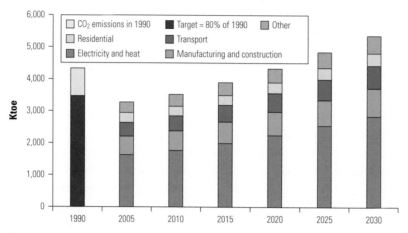

Source: Data for 1990 and 2005 are from IEA 2007b; data for 2010–30 are World Bank staff projections.

Policies and Instruments for Reducing Carbon Emissions

Policymakers and businesses must rethink their national energy strategies and seriously engage in global efforts to reduce carbon emissions. Demands for carbon reductions will only grow, and the region must do its share. But moving to a low-carbon economy can be costly, depending on the targets. Many policy options and instruments, including the following, can help the region reduce its carbon footprint and attract the capital to rebuild its energy infrastructure and industrial base using more efficient and cleaner technologies:

- Global partnerships
- Cap-and-trade instruments
- The Global Environment Facility
- The Climate Investment Fund
- Carbon taxes
- Technical standards and labeling
- Fuel switching.

This section explores these possibilities. But dealing with the region's environmental conundrum will require looking beyond policies narrowly defined for climate change.

Global Partnerships

With the EU Emissions Trading Scheme and the Kyoto Protocol, countries committed to reducing carbon emissions and mitigating climate change. Most countries in the region ratified the Kyoto Protocol, which distinguishes two groups of countries. Annex 1 countries (industrial countries) have a target of reducing their collective greenhouse gas emissions by 5.2 percent below the 1990 baseline in 2008–12. Non–Annex 1 countries (developing countries) have no greenhouse gas reduction targets.

The European Union has taken the lead in promoting an ambitious framework for climate policy, seeking to improve energy security, accelerate innovation, and gain a competitive edge in clean energy and industrial technologies. The new Energy Policy for Europe will affect energy and climate policies among the region's EU members and aspiring members. The EU goals are to reduce greenhouse gas emissions by 20 percent, obtain 20 percent of energy from renewable sources, and improve energy efficiency by 20 percent. The expected cost is 0.58 percent of GDP, or $139 billion in 2020. These policies would cut energy intensity about 32 percent between 2005 and 2020.[2] The goals would be flexible for new members Bulgaria and Romania, which would be allowed to increase emissions up to 20 percent over 2005 levels by 2020 while their economies converge to those of the EU25.

Harmonization with EU legislation is already taking place. The Hungarian Parliament adopted a program to promote renewable energy; the new Czech Energy Management Act created the basis for raising energy efficiency in line with the EU energy *acquis*.[3] Competition, cost savings, and pressure to keep up with EU standards have steadily driven down energy intensity in the accession countries, with energy consumption and greenhouse gas emissions per GDP declining in all Central and Eastern European states. Croatia and Hungary are the best performers, registering energy intensities within 30 percent of the EU average. Belarus has shown that energy intensity can be addressed quickly, having reduced its energy intensity by more than 50 percent between 1997 and 2008. But most of the region lags behind. Many countries have not enacted significant legislation to reduce their climate impact.

Cap-and-Trade Instruments

A number of different approaches have been developed to finance the reduction of emissions. These include a variety of cap-and-trade instruments, which complement other sources of funds, such as the Global Environment Facility and the Clean Technology Fund.

The Kyoto Protocol

The Kyoto Protocol gives Annex 1 countries three flexible mechanisms to achieve compliance in the first commitment period (2008–12):

- *International emissions trading.* Assigned amount units (AAUs) can be traded among Annex B countries (that is, the emissions-capped industrial countries and transition economies listed in Annex B of Article 17 of the Kyoto Protocol).

- *Joint implementation.* Annex 1 countries can purchase emissions reductions from projects in other Annex 1 countries under Article 6.[4]

- *The clean development mechanism.* Annex 1 countries can purchase certified emission reductions from projects in developing countries (not parties to Annex 1) under Article 12.

Project-based transactions under joint implementation or the clean development mechanism create an opportunity for host countries to leverage foreign investment, promote the transfer of efficient technologies and best practices, and contribute to long-term climate change mitigation and sustainable development. For investors, they are a cost-effective alternative to domestic reductions. The rationale for joint implementation is that Annex 1 countries with high marginal costs for CO_2 reductions will benefit from investing in other Annex 1 countries with lower costs. The European Union's Linking Directive allows a portion of the credits from joint implementation and the clean development mechanism to be used to comply with its emission trading scheme.[5]

These mechanisms have great potential to improve energy efficiency, promote carbon capture, and create new generating capacity based on renewable energy. Given the mounting interest in projects to reduce gas flaring and venting, the region's energy producers may be able to tap carbon finance to bring to market a portion of the estimated 71 billion cubic meters of natural gas—12.5 percent of EU25 gas consumption—currently flared or vented into the atmosphere, causing greenhouse gas emissions of almost 200 million tons (Baugh et al. 2007; see also chapter 3). So far the countries in the region have not taken advantage of this potential.

International emissions trading. The World Bank estimates that through the clean development mechanism and joint implementation, industrial countries can trade carbon emissions of 300 million tons between 2008 and 2012 (World Bank 2004). This leaves a compliance gap of 700 million tons a year, making the countries in the region candidates to sell the remainder. Potential sellers exploring opportunities include Bulgaria, the Czech Republic, Hungary, Latvia, Romania, Russia, and Ukraine. It is estimated that the region owns more than 7 billion tons of tradable surplus allowances (Point Carbon 2007).

Future prices for AAUs are unpredictable, but estimates place them at $6–$12 ton. The potential financing is thus substantial, but significant barriers to AAU trading remain. Potential sovereign buyers are concerned that transfers are not "additional" and have expressed interest in international emissions trading only if AAUs are linked to investment in climate-friendly programs (called green investment schemes). And AAU holders may decide not to trade the allowance, using it instead to compensate for their own carbon emissions trajectories. Estimates of the market value of these allowances range from $7 billion to $24 billion. If this capital becomes available, it could bring substantial resources to countries in the region implementing green investment schemes.

Joint implementation. Joint implementation has a mixed record in the region. Between 2003 and 2006, the market was dominated by Russia (21 percent), Ukraine (20 percent), and Bulgaria (19 percent), with significant activity in Hungary, Poland, and Estonia as well. Russia and Ukraine are key, with the potential to deliver more than 1.5 billion tons of CO_2 reduction. But because of incomplete reforms to the legal framework, institutional barriers, and bureaucracy, Russia and other countries in the region have yet to issue the letters of approval necessary for successful joint implementation arrangements.

The Clean Development Mechanism. The Clean Development Mechanism has only limited penetration in the region. In 2006 non-Annex I countries in the region participated in 34 projects, or 1.2 percent of the total, creating 3,541 certified emissions reductions. Moldova has been particularly active, gaining practical experience in promoting carbon projects. Its projects—efficiency improvements and fuel switching for public buildings—are expected to reduce greenhouse gas emissions by about 11 million tons a year. The South Caucasus region has projects for reducing methane from landfills, with large potential for carbon financing for reducing gas leaks from pipelines and upstream installations. But it takes time and effort to gain market experience, foster institutional reforms, and acquire technology and expertise, and much more could be traded.

The EU Emission Trading Scheme
The most prominent regional arrangement for emissions trading, the EU emission trading scheme, is a viable instrument for abating

emissions. Emissions allowances are actively traded to comply with mandates and exploit financial or hedging opportunities. The scheme allows importing into the system credits from joint implementation and the clean development mechanism. It limits the greenhouse gases that industry and power generation may emit. The scheme covers about 11,000 sources of emission, primarily power plants and energy-intensive industries, which are collectively responsible for nearly half of EU emissions of CO_2 and 40 percent of total EU emissions. The scheme will boost cost-efficient reductions of greenhouse gases and demonstrate the synergies between the scheme and renewable policies (European Commission 2008).

The second phase of the EU climate strategy focuses on strengthening the emissions trading scheme, tackling emissions from aviation and passenger road transport, developing carbon capture and storage technology, and identifying adaptation measures. Based on these goals, the European Commission has proposed legislation to include airlines in the trading scheme and to cut greenhouse gas emissions from road fuels. It has also announced legislation to reduce CO_2 emissions from new cars. Proposals for phase 3 of the trading scheme are being negotiated for 2013–20.

The Global Environmental Facility

Since 1991, the Global Environmental Facility (GEF) has been an important funder of projects designed to improve the global environment in the CSE/CIS region. The GEF provides grants to finance projects in climate change mitigation, by reducing or avoiding greenhouse gas emissions through renewable energy, energy efficiency, and sustainable transport, and in climate change adaptation, by aiming to increase resilience to the adverse impacts of climate change of vulnerable countries, sectors, and communities. GEF resources have been useful in building capacity and piloting new technologies.

The Climate Investment Funds

The Climate Investment Funds (CIFs) can finance carbon reduction activities in the CSE/CIS region. They are multidonor trust funds, launched at the 2008 G8 summit. CIF resources (of $6.3 billion) are available through the multilateral development banks to assist developing countries fill financing gaps to support efforts to mitigate or strengthen resilience to the impacts of climate change. The CIF opens the opportunity for blending funding from multilateral development banks and national and private sector development resources, thereby leveraging substantial additional funds.

The two CIF funds are the Clean Technology Fund (CTF), which finances scaled-up demonstration, deployment, and transfer of low-carbon technologies for significant greenhouse gas reductions within country investment plans, and the Strategic Climate Fund (SCF), which finances targeted programs in developing countries to pilot new climate or sectoral approaches with scaling-up potential. Three CTF programs have been initiated in the CSE/CIS region, in Kazakhstan, Turkey, and Ukraine.

Carbon Taxes

Carbon taxes could complement carbon trading as a tool for mitigating climate change. One merit of carbon taxes is that they normally lend predictability to energy prices. Cap-and-trade systems can exacerbate volatility, discouraging investments in less carbon-intensive electricity generation, carbon-reducing energy efficiency, and carbon-replacing renewable energy. Carbon taxes tend to be less vulnerable to market uncertainties and provide clear price signals, both of which could encourage investment. Carbon taxes should therefore be considered as another instrument in the design of energy policies in the region.

Taxes on gasoline are already widespread. In addition, governments could levy a tax on the upstream production of coal, oil, and gas, gradually raising the price of energy from fossil fuels to include the full cost of the environmental impact. The cost of coal would increase more than that of other energy sources, because it emits more CO_2 for each unit of energy. The cost of natural gas would rise by less. Such taxation would incentivize investors to design cleaner electricity-generating plants, refurbish outdated energy infrastructure, and switch to cleaner technologies. It would encourage consumers to be more energy efficient.

Another advantage of carbon taxes is that they can be designed and implemented rapidly, with less cost and institutional complexity than cap-and-trade systems. However, public backing for a tax may be weaker than for cap-and-trade arrangements. Carbon taxes can also address greenhouse gas emissions for all sectors; cap-and-trade systems have primarily targeted the power industry. The tax revenues generated could be used to offset other taxes to compensate lower-income households and minimize damage to the economy. Revenues from auctioning off emission permits could be used in the same way.

Both taxation and cap-and-trade schemes raise the cost of CO_2 emissions but in very different ways. Carbon taxes directly—and predictably—influence price. Cap-and-trade schemes control quantity. By fixing the quantity of greenhouse gas emissions, such schemes drive price adjustments to meet that ceiling. Critics of cap-and-trade argue that quotas exacerbate price fluctuations, affecting business investment and household consumption. Carbon trading provides limited price signals (five to eight a year), because of frequent climate negotiations, making it difficult to price carbon into decisions about long-lived assets and long-term technology development. It may be impossible to negotiate an internationally equitable carbon tax, and some countries may choose to free-ride in order to boost their relative competitiveness. This could lead other countries to retaliate with import duties based on the relative carbon footprint of imported goods, including electricity.

Technical Standards and Labeling

Technical standards are another set of instruments to control emissions. An example is the European standard defining the acceptable limit for exhaust emissions from new vehicles sold in member states (figure 5.4). The standards are defined in a series of EU directives that introduce progressively more stringent standards. NOx, hydrocarbons, carbon monoxide, and particulate matter are regulated for motor vehicle types. Although CO_2 emissions from transport have risen rapidly in recent years—from 21 percent of the total in 1990 to 28 percent in 2004—there are no standards for CO_2 emissions from vehicles. In 2007, however, the European Commission published draft legislation to limit average CO_2 emissions from

FIGURE 5.4

NOx and Particulate Matter Standards for New Gasoline Vehicles Sold in the European Union, 1992–2005

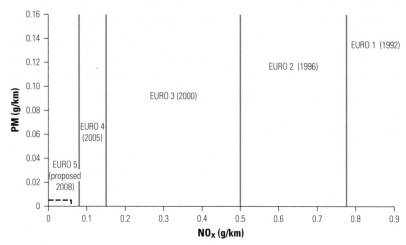

Source: http://en.wikipedia.org/wiki/Image:Euronorms_Petrol.png.

the European fleet of cars to 120 grams per kilometer. Other examples of technical standards include facility-specific pollution control requirements, limits on emissions per kilowatt hour of electricity generated, fuel economy requirements for new vehicles, and regulations on fuels.

Based on cost-effectiveness (the lowest cost per ton of emissions reductions), market-based instruments such as carbon taxes and emissions trading are typically superior to traditional regulation. Market policies equalize the marginal cost of abatement across all sectors, firms, and abatement opportunities, with the least expensive (substituting less carbon-intensive fuels, adopting energy-efficient technologies, conserving household energy by driving less, and reducing residential heating and cooling loads) implemented first.

Traditional regulations are nevertheless frequently proposed as alternatives or complements to emissions taxes or tradable permits. They include technology standards that dictate a particular technology or method and performance standards that limit emissions per unit of economic output or activity. Economic analyses reach uniformly negative conclusions about the cost-effectiveness of traditional regulations as alternatives to emissions taxes or tradable permits. There is an economic argument for performance standards that complement a market-based carbon regime. Performance standards may be necessary to address market failures. For example, consumers may undervalue more energy-efficient vehicles or appliances. Developing new technologies may also generate substantial public benefits—in new knowledge—that the firm conducting the research does not capture. Alternatively, the inability to price emissions reductions appropriately may reflect political opposition to higher energy prices and concerns about the international competitiveness of energy-intensive industries.

Economies that have successfully reduced greenhouse gas emissions have demonstrated that standards play an important role in achieving results. A related instrument is clear labeling of the carbon emissions caused by the production of goods and services, which provides consumers with the informational basis for making their own choices.

Fuel Switching

The region's substantial contribution to global warming largely reflects its high energy intensity and high carbon intensity. The causes? Outmoded generation technology and reliance on coal.

Fuel switching means replacing high-carbon fuels with low-carbon fuels. The switch is already taking place in Central and Eastern Europe, where the Kyoto Protocol's joint implementation provisions have catalyzed renewable energy projects. In general terms, though, the region's renewable energy development is underfunded, and several governments remain unpersuaded of the profitability of renewable energy projects or the environmental benefit deriving from such projects.

Some countries in the region, especially those heavily reliant on energy imports, have started to promote renewable domestic sources, such as wind, geothermal, and solar power. In 2008 the annual growth rates for wind energy were 178 percent in Bulgaria, 95 percent in Hungary, and 71 percent in Poland (World Wind Energy Association 2009). Poland has been one of the most receptive countries, because of state support and the availability of land. It may have as much as 13 gigawatts of renewable installed capacity by 2020 (Cardais 2008).

The cost of alternative energy is rapidly falling and may soon be fully competitive with traditional power generation (figure 5.5). The cost of wind power has been brought down to about $.10 per kWh of electricity, and the latest photovoltaic solar power systems promise

FIGURE 5.5

Cost of Abating Emissions

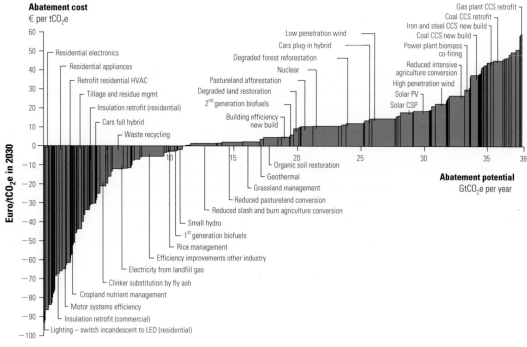

Source: McKinsey & Company 2009.

Note: The curve presents an estimate of the maximum potential of all technical GHG abatement measures below €60 per tCO_2e if each lever was pursued aggressively. It is not a forecast of what role different abatement measures and technologies will play.

to reduce the cost to less than $.30 per kWh (for a fully integrated system incorporating storage).

Several other energy sources can limit emissions. These include a number of renewable energy sources, outlined below.

Wind Power

Foreign investments in wind power in Central European countries had been increasing before the financial crisis hit and can be expected to emerge once the crisis is past. In addition, the European Union, through its Cohesion Fund, aims to provide several billion dollars in subsidies for renewable energy projects in new member countries. In Bulgaria, the Czech Republic, Hungary, Romania, and the Slovak Republic, combined installed capacity reached 447 megawatts in 2008. In Turkey the calculated wind power capacity has been reported as 48 gigawatts; existing installed capacity is only 333 megawatts. The wind energy successes in these countries and partly in Ukraine have occurred thanks to strong government commitments to renewable energy. These countries have encouraged renewable energy investment by implementing a feed-in tariff scheme for wind and biomass that forces national utilities to buy electricity from renewable energy producers (sometimes at above-market prices), basically guaranteeing a revenue stream for the producers.

Solar Power

Solar power generation has not experienced deep penetration in the region. Its use so far has been limited to solar collectors used to heat water, and even that has not penetrated many markets, despite a suitable weather belt for using significant solar energy. The potential is well distributed throughout the region. In Turkey alone the solar energy potential for heating purposes is estimated at 36 Mtoe. Photovoltaic electricity generation is yet to have much impact, primarily because of its high cost and the lack of adequate regulatory regimes. However, it is expected that current costs will continue to decline, especially as a result of significantly increased production volumes. Countries such as Hungary, Poland, and Turkey, which are already exploring solar power potential, will be well positioned to benefit from these developments. Other countries in the region should follow suit.

Geothermal Power

Geothermal electricity generation has recently been developed in many countries in the region. One of the countries with the largest potential is Russia, which could use modern geothermal technology to reduce its dependence on hydrocarbons for power generation.

Hungary has the most significant geothermal potential in Eastern Europe; Poland also has good geothermal possibilities.

Turkey is the seventh-richest country in the world in geothermal energy potential. It has 172 geothermal regions over 300°C. Their total potential is estimated at 31 gigawatts, only about 4 percent of which is used efficiently.

Biomass

Many countries in the region have large agriculture sectors. Their potential to produce biomass for power generation and fuels could therefore be substantial. However, the investment potential is currently unknown.

European biofuel producers are investing heavily in Latvia, Romania, Ukraine, and other Eastern European countries. There are possibilities for further growth in the biomass sector in countries with large forest and agricultural sectors, such as Belarus, Bulgaria, the Czech Republic, Hungary, Lithuania, Poland, and Romania. However, moving extensively to biofuels can lead to higher food prices, with strongly negative impact on consumers, especially the poor. Using arable land for the production of biofuels makes little economic sense in the countries in the region.

Hydropower

The region's technically exploitable hydropower potential amounts to 2,646 TWh a year, of which only about 13 percent is being used. This potential is concentrated in three countries. About 63 percent (1,670 TWh a year) is in Russia. The only other countries with significant exploitable potential are Tajikistan (264 TWh/year) and Turkey (216 TWh/year). Most countries in the region use much less than half their technically exploitable potential. Increasing hydropower may, however, become riskier as a result of climate change, which is causing greater volatility in weather patterns and prolonged droughts.

Nuclear Power

Generation of nuclear power is expected to triple between 2005 and 2030, with new generation in countries with existing facilities (Bulgaria, Romania, Russia, and Ukraine). Also likely are new projects supported by a consortium of countries, as in a new plant to include Poland and Latvia as investors and Lithuania as the host country and operator. The region has substantial uranium reserves to fuel the new plants, concentrated in Kazakhstan, Russia, Ukraine, and Uzbekistan. Total regional reserves account for 26 percent of global reserves, equivalent to just over 100 years of regional production in 2005. Regional production was 26 percent of the global total. Special attention must be given to ensure that both regulations and operational practices are satisfactory at all stages of the nuclear lifecycle, from the mining of the uranium to the disposal of the nuclear waste.

Integrating Environmental Protection across Sectors

Oil, gas, and mining create local and regional environmental risks and global threats from climate change. Well-governed sectors can deal with the present and future environmental impacts and address the liabilities from the region's history. The region's governments, through their environmental and regulatory agencies and, for state-owned companies, owners' representatives, should take the following steps:

- Ensure that all energy operations—oil, gas, and coal production; storage, transmission, and transport; heat and power generation units; and nuclear and hydropower plants—take place in an environmentally acceptable and sustainable manner.
- Stop gas flaring and venting.
- Upgrade aging refineries and stop seepage.
- Clean up legacy oil contamination of land and water.
- Give special attention to ensuring that regulations and operational practices are satisfactory at all stages of the nuclear lifecycle, from mining uranium to disposing of nuclear waste.
- Include the costs of environmental damage in the cost of energy.

Coal accounts for only 20 percent of the region's energy production but 36 percent of its emissions. Many countries in the region plan to increase coal-fired power generation considerably. The growth in carbon emissions could nevertheless slow if new power generators and rehabilitated units use high-efficiency technologies, such as the integrated gasification combined cycle or ultra-super-critical pulverized coal technology. But the savings would be modest. Carbon capture and storage could become possible between 2020 and 2030, once feasibility and costs are established for specific locations. Progress will also depend on identifying suitable sealable saline aquifers to store the carbon.

Governments of countries that use coal heavily or are shifting to coal should implement measures to reduce the growth of greenhouse gas emissions. Possible measures include the following:

- Reduce coal-based carbon emissions by providing incentives or mandates for rehabilitating and modernizing coal-based power plants and upgrading power plant combustion technologies (for example, pulverized coal and integrated combined cycle gasification, super-critical and ultra-super critical).

- Create incentives or mandate that coal mining companies upgrade their coal supplies (higher-quality hard coal produces lower carbon emissions per kilowatt generated than lower-quality lignite).

- Put in place mechanisms and procedures to use carbon finance to help meet emissions targets or to "buy down" emissions impacts.

- Support research and development by providing incentives for power plant operators to undertake pilot applications of new technologies, including carbon capture and storage.

- Ensure that new technologies to minimize greenhouse gases from coal, once available and affordable, are implemented, at least in locations with access to deep-seated, structurally sound saline aquifers.

There is a disconnect between global efforts to reduce carbon emissions and the region's national energy strategies for the next 20 years. The region's policymakers and businesses must rethink these strategies and engage seriously in global efforts. Demands for carbon reductions will only intensify, especially with the EU requirements for a 20 percent reduction by 2020.

The countries of the region should take the following steps:

- Participate actively in global partnerships on climate change and greenhouse gas reduction.

- Incorporate carbon reduction in national energy strategies.

- Harmonize emissions legislation, standards, and enforcement with international standards to overcome any credibility gap.

- Establish the institutional and technical capacity to trade on the carbon market.

- Use carbon financing to leverage the large, urgent modernization of their energy infrastructure at all levels.

- Consider carbon taxes as an alternative to other taxes.

- Encourage fuel switching to clean energy, including by setting up a regulatory framework for decentralized alternative energy production.

The Need to Embrace Mitigation and Adaptation

All countries in the region will need to embrace practical mitigation and adaptation strategies for greenhouse gas emissions and global warming. Tackling carbon emissions project by project is unlikely to deliver the large-scale, long-term investments necessary to reduce the region's climate impact. New approaches are thus needed. The array of

TABLE 5.1

Policy Instruments for Addressing Adaptation to and Mitigation of Problems of Greenhouse Gas Emissions and Global Warming

Feature	Carbon tax	Cap-and-trade	Traditional regulation
Certainty about CO_2 prices	Yes; tax establishes a well-defined price.	No; but price volatility can be limited by design features, such as a safety valve (price cap) or borrowing.	No
Certainty over emissions	No; emissions vary with prevailing energy demand and fuel prices.	Yes, in its traditional form (capped emission sources). No, with the use of additional cost-containment mechanisms.	No; regulating rate of emissions leaves level uncertain.
Efficiently encourages least-cost emissions reductions	Yes	Yes	No; but tradable standards are more efficient than nontradable standards.
Ability to raise revenue	Yes; results in maximum revenue generation compared with other options (assuming the cap-and-trade alternative includes substantial free allocation of allowances).	Traditionally—with a largely free allocation—no. Growing interest in a substantial allowance auction suggests an opportunity to raise at least some revenue now and possibly transition to a complete auction that generates maximum revenue in the future.	No
Incentives for research and development in clean technologies	Yes; stable CO_2 price is needed to induce innovation.	Yes; however, uncertainty over permit prices could weaken innovation incentives.	Yes and no; standards encourage specific technologies but not broad innovation.
Harm to competitiveness	Yes; although if other taxes are reduced through revenue recycling, competitiveness of the broader economy can be improved.	Yes (as with a tax); but giving firms free allowances offsets potentially harmful effect on profitability.	Somewhat; regulations increase the cost of manufacturing but, unlike taxes or tradable permits, do not raise the price of fossil energy.
Practical or political obstacles to implementation	Yes; new taxes have been very unpopular.	Yes; identifying a reasonable allocation and target is difficult.	Yes; setting level of standard is difficult.
New institutional requirements	Minimal	Yes; but experience with existing trading programs suggests that markets (for trading permits and exchanging information across firms and time periods) arise quickly and relatively inexpensively.	Minimal (unless tradable)

Source: Parry and Pizer 2007.

policies and instruments—cap-and-trade, carbon taxes, public investment policies, standards, market incentives, and regulations—should be incorporated into the region's national energy strategies. Also needed are stronger global partnerships and agreements. Table 5.1 summarizes key features of some of these policy instruments. In addition, an effective energy efficiency program with broad penetration is needed, as described earlier.

Notes

1. Estonia's carbon intensity probably reflects its heavy reliance on oil shale.
2. These objectives are projected to be reached at a carbon price of €39 per ton of CO_2 and a renewable energy incentive of €45 per MWh. Oil and gas imports are expected to fall by some €50 billion in 2020, air pollution control costs to drop by about €10 billion in 2020, and electricity prices to go up by 10–15 percent relative to 2005 levels.
3. The EU *acquis*, or *acquis communautaire*, refers to the total body of EU law created to date.
4. About 95 percent of projects of this type take place in transition economies.
5. Unlike the first phase, which ended in a low and volatile carbon price, the second phase has already created a relatively stable carbon price, a vibrant link with the Clean Development Mechanism market, and numerous new financial products.

CHAPTER 6

Creating an Enabling Environment for Investment

The total projected energy sector investment requirements for the region over the next 20–25 years are huge. They amount to about $3.3 trillion (in 2008 dollars), some 3 percent of accumulated GDP during that period (table 6.1).

Although the public sector will have to finance a portion of these investments, it will not have the capacity to meet the full investment needs. The countries in the region will therefore need to call on the financial depth and technical know-how of private sector investors and energy companies. Although the current financial crisis is a serious impediment to private sector investment in any activities or countries seen as high risk, as the financial crisis passes, the prospects for such investment will improve. However, in order to attract these investors, countries will need to create an enabling environment that provides secure ownership rights, is subject to the rule of law, fosters transparency, and enables reasonable risk mitigation. In addition, individual sectors will have to be viewed as financially and commercially viable. This will be particularly critical in those sectors, such as electricity and heat, that are largely dependent on their domestic markets.

TABLE 6.1

Total Projected Energy Sector Investment Needed in the Region by 2030–35, by Subsector

(billions of 2008 dollars)

Subsector	Investment required
Electricity	1,500
Crude oil	900
Heating	500
Gas	230
Coal	150
Refining	20
Total	3,300

Source: World Bank staff calculations.

Creating an Attractive Business Environment

In order to create an attractive environment for investment, countries will need to adhere to a number of key principles (7 "do's" and 3 "don'ts"), grouped here under 10 headings. Although these principles are not equally important, all have significant bearing on perceptions of the overall climate for investment. Government actions that are consistent with these principles will go a long way toward creating an attractive and competitive investment climate in the energy sector.

1. Do not impose a punitive or regressive tax regime. An underlying principle of effective taxation is that, to the greatest extent possible, the tax system should ensure that projects with pretax (or economic) rates of return should show positive post tax (or financial) rates of return as well. A tax system that produces this result is called "neutral." Full neutrality may be difficult to achieve, but it remains an important tax objective. The concept of progressive taxation, in which there is a positive correlation between government take and underlying project profitability, is a widely accepted approach, particularly in the petroleum sector (box 6.1). A regressive system of taxation, in which the government's percentage share of the economic rent increases as profitability declines, should be avoided.

2. Do introduce an acceptable legal framework. An acceptable legal framework protects the interests of both the state and investors (box 6.2). Its main purposes are to provide the basic context for and rules governing operations in the energy subsectors in the host country; regulate energy operations as they are carried out by both domestic and foreign enterprises; and define the principal administrative, economic, and fiscal guidelines for investment activity in the energy subsectors.

BOX 6.1

Components of an Effective Tax System for the Petroleum Sector

Tax payments may be made in cash or in kind (in-kind payments are common under production sharing arrangements). Regardless of the form of payment, certain characteristics are common to tax systems that achieve the dual objectives of offering competitive tax terms to investors and ensuring that the state receives an equitable share of the economic rent from its hydrocarbon resources. An acceptable tax package for oil production might include the following components:

- A reasonable royalty, which provides the state with an assured return for permitting the investor to exploit its hydrocarbon resources.

- A corporate profits tax with reasonable cost-recovery provisions. The tax rate should be the same as that applied to corporate profits generally.

- An additional profits tax tied to actual profitability, which can be used to capture "excess profits," thereby increasing government revenues without adversely affecting economically desirable investment decisions.

Reasonable business expenses should be deductible for tax purposes. The definition of such expenses should be applied consistently across the industry, in a fashion that reflects the true economic costs to the business.

BOX 6.2

A Legal Framework for the Petroleum Sector

The essential elements of a legal framework for the petroleum sector are a petroleum law, enabling regulations, and one of several variants of a model contract. Such a framework should provide both the host country and investors with a clear legal and contractual context within which to negotiate exploration and production arrangements that are mutually advantageous and will lead to development of the petroleum resources of the host state. The fiscal and tax aspects of a complete petroleum legislative framework can either be detailed in the petroleum law itself or set out in a companion petroleum revenue code, either of which could complete the legislative package.

---

3. Do provide supporting regulations, administered by an independent and impartial regulator. Regulations are an essential component of successful energy legislation. They should provide the detail and procedures needed to implement the policy and meet the objectives of the energy legislation.

Establishing policy is the responsibility of the government and the legislature. The role of the regulator is simply to administer the regulations arising from that policy. The regulator should, therefore, be independent of the policy-making process.

Regulation of the power sector varies across countries in the region (table 6.2). Countries that are EU members or have EU aspirations generally show the most progress.

TABLE 6.2

Status of Regulatory Institutions in the Region by November 2008, by Country

		Separate regulator	Fixed-term appointment	Industry funding	Full tariff setting power	Transparency	Right to appeal
South East Europe	Albania	✓	✓	✓	✓	✓	✓
	Bosnia & Herzegovina	✓	✓	✓	✓	✓	✓
	Croatia	✓	✓	✓	✗	✓	✓
	FYR Macedonia	✓	✓	✓	✓	✓	✓
	Montenegro	✓	✓	✓	✗	✓	✓
	Serbia	✓	✓	✓	✗	✗	✓
EU Countries	Bulgaria	✓	✓	✓	✗	✓	✓
	Czech Republic	✓	✓	✗	✗	✓	✓
	Estonia	✓	✗	✗	✓	✓	✓
	Hungary	✓	✓	✓	✗	✓	✓
	Latvia	✓	✓	✓	✓	✓	✗
	Lithuania	✓	✓	✗	✓	✓	✓
	Poland	✓	✓	✗	✓	✗	✓
	Romania	✓	✓	✓	✓	✓	✓
	Slovak Republic	✓	✓	✗	✓	✓	✗
	Slovenia	✓	✓	✓	✓	✓	✗
Black Sea & Belarus	Armenia	✓	✗	✗	✓	✓	✗
	Belarus	✗	✗	✗	✗	✗	✗
	Georgia	✓	✓	✓	✓	✓	✓
	Moldova	✓	✓	✓	✓	✓	✓
	Ukraine	✓	✓	✗	✓	✓	✗
	Turkey	✓	✓	✓	✓	✓	✗
Caspian & Central Asia	Azerbaijan	✓	✗	✗	✗	✗	✓
	Kazakhstan	✓	✗	✗	✓	✓	✓
	Kyrgyz Republic	✓	✓	✗	✓	✗	✓
	Tajikistan	✗	✗	✗	✗	✗	✗
	Uzbekistan	✓					
	Turkmenistan	✗	✗	✗	✗	✗	✗

Source: Bank staff based on ERRA 2008.

4. Do create an environment that facilitates assured nondiscriminatory access to markets. Creating such an environment involves providing access to both domestic and international markets (if applicable), providing access to existing transportation facilities (on a non-discriminatory basis), and making it possible for investors to establish new transportation options. In host countries in which transportation options are limited, perceptions concerning access to markets play a very significant role in risk assessment by potential investors.

5. Do not interfere with the functioning of the marketplace. Examples of interference with the functioning of the marketplace include state orders related to the delivery of crude oil and refined products, pricing controls, and restrictions on the import and export of energy products.

6. Do not discriminate among investors. Not only should host countries avoid discrimination among investors, they should avoid even the perception of such discrimination. Measures to avoid discrimination include the following:

- Pursuing open and transparent processes for the award of licenses, contracts, and concessions
- Enacting legislation to preclude discrimination (and providing the full support of the judicial system to enforce this legislation)
- Ensuring that the laws and regulations affecting the sector are consistently applied.

One additional factor that can come into play is differences between practices in a particular host country and normal international practice and the way the government addresses those differences. If, for example, certain investors are able to get away with such actions as ignoring internationally accepted environmental and safety standards, not paying taxes, and bribing officials, the effect will be a climate that discriminates against the investor that fully complies with internationally accepted standards.

7. Do honor internationally accepted standards. Examples of internationally accepted standards that should be honored include using international accounting standards, allowing investors to have recourse to international arbitration, and honoring the provisions of international treaties.

8. Do abide by contractual undertakings, and preclude the use of an administrative bureaucracy to constrain investor activities. Abiding by contractual undertakings requires governments to introduce "grandfathering" provisions when laws change in order to ensure that the negotiated terms of existing contracts are protected. Red tape is a major impediment to investment; delays translate into lower returns. In the petroleum sector, for example, the recommended approach is to empower a single government entity (or competent authority) to implement policy in petroleum development. Such an authority can be used to resolve disputes involving petroleum investors and other government agencies.

9. Do prevent monopoly abuses. Monopoly abuses can emanate from national companies in the energy sector, from dominant players in the market place, from holders of "natural monopolies" (such as pipeline or power transmission companies), and from key service providers, such as power and water utilities. Regulatory oversight of monopolies may be required to prevent monopoly abuses.

10. Do ensure that the sector is kept free of corruption. Corruption is a major impediment to economic development. With its large financial flows, the energy sector is a tempting target for corruption.

Eliminating corruption is a complex process that takes both time and the absolute commitment of a country's leaders. Elements of an anticorruption program include the following:

- *Economic reform.* Adoption of sound development strategies creates an environment of hope in the future of the economy as a whole. The loss of such hope contributes to a shift toward corrupt practices for many of those who see in them the only chance for improving their own conditions.

- *Legal and judicial reform.* Clarifying and streamlining necessary laws, eliminating unnecessary laws, and strengthening the law enforcement capacity while putting in place an efficient and just judicial process are general steps for the creation of a sound investment climate. They are also necessary for reducing the incidence of corruption.

- *Administrative reform.* Reform of the civil service should make it responsive to actual needs. A key component of civil service reform (which also applies to the judiciary) is to provide adequate remuneration, reducing—and ideally eliminating—the need for public employees to take illicit bribes.

These reforms should be supplemented by the introduction of adequate checks and balances.

Ensuring the Financial and Commercial Viability of the Sector

For those segments of the energy sector that can secure ready access to international markets (for example, oil production), financial viability is dictated largely by market conditions, although it can be undermined by inappropriate fiscal policies. For those segments of the sector that depend on the domestic market—notably energy utilities—financial viability is dictated by the conditions prevalent within those markets.

During the Soviet period, utility services such as electricity were provided at tariffs that were considerably below full cost-recovery levels; state enterprises relied on budget support for their continued existence and provision of services. Low tariffs and the associated culture of state support led to high levels of energy consumption and to significant operational inefficiencies that have persisted across much of the region. These inefficiencies include weak payment discipline, high levels of technical losses, and tariffs set below full cost recovery levels. Ensuring that utilities function on a financially sustainable basis, without being a drain on the state's budget, requires addressing these three problem areas.

Strengthening Payment Discipline

Strengthening payment discipline—the extent to which consumers pay for energy utility services—is a critical first step toward improving the financial viability of the energy utility service sectors, because it is a key determinant of the sectors' revenues. Doing so requires improving collection rates and addressing commercial losses, which can result, for example, from theft and the use of artificial norms that understate consumption.

Experience in the region has demonstrated that success in improving payment discipline depends fundamentally on the willingness of governments to introduce some key measures:

- Amending relevant laws that allow utilities to recover amounts due from customers in a timely fashion and to deny service to those who do not pay their bills

- Ensuring that public sector users (such as government departments and agencies) have adequate earmarked budget provisions to pay their utility bills and subjecting them to the discipline of disconnection for nonpayment

- Making theft of services a criminal offence, with associated deterrent punishments.

FIGURE 6.1

Average Collection Rates in the Region, 1995–2008

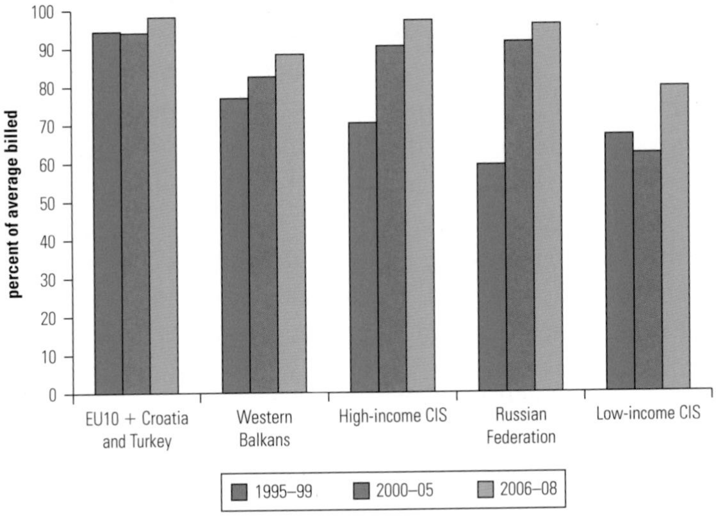

Source: EBRD 2008.

Improving Collections

Countries in Central and Eastern Europe introduced measures to improve collections relatively early in the transition period and were able to improve collection rates in a relatively short period of time. By the mid-1990s, the average collection rate in Bulgaria, Hungary, Lithuania, and Poland was already about 90 percent (figure 6.1). Since then the situation in the EU member states in the region has continued to improve and is now close to 100 percent.

Collection rates have also been improving in other countries in the region. However, challenges remain, particularly in Albania, Azerbaijan, the Kyrgyz Republic, Kosovo, FYR Macedonia, and Uzbekistan, where weak governance is emerging as one of the barriers to improving collections. Throughout the region, the legal framework needs strengthening to allow utilities to disconnect federal, provincial, and municipal agencies and facilities that fail to meet their payment obligations. In many countries, there are still long lists of public agencies and facilities that cannot be disconnected for nonpayment on the grounds that they perform a nationally important function or that disconnection would cause serious harm or production losses. If this is the case, these agencies and facilities should be allocated adequate funds to meet their service payment obligations.

Reducing Technical Losses

Technical losses for energy utility supplies remain high in the region. For electricity, they average about twice the OECD levels. Consolidated

TABLE 6.3

Total Technical and Commercial Losses in CSE/CIS Economies

Percentage loss	Economies
< 8	EU-15, Czech Republic, Slovak Republic, Slovenia
9–11	Bulgaria, Estonia, Hungary, Lithuania, Poland, Romania, Russian Federation
12–14	Armenia, Azerbaijan, Belarus, Georgia, Turkey, Turkmenistan, Ukraine
15–17	Bosnia and Herzegovina, Croatia, Latvia, Serbia
20–30	Kazakhstan, Kyrgyz Republic, FYR Macedonia, Montenegro, Tajikistan, Uzbekistan
> 35	Albania, Kosovo, Moldova

Source: For Kazakhstan, Kosovo, Kyrgyz Republic, Tajikistan, and Uzbekistan: Bank staff. For Montenegro: IEA 2008b. For all other countries: World Bank Development database 2007b.

technical and commercial losses in the power transmission and distribution networks show a wide range, from less than 8 percent in many of the region's EU countries to more than 35 percent in Albania, Kosovo, and Moldova (table 6.3).

Improvements should result over time, as assets are retired and replaced by new assets. In the short and medium term, technical losses can be reduced by rehabilitating and reinforcing the transmission and distribution systems.

Setting Tariffs to Recover Full Costs

A critical element required to ensure the financial viability of utility companies is setting and maintaining tariffs at levels that will provide for full cost recovery. Tariffs must be high enough to cover the cost of inputs and operating and maintenance costs as well as provide for the recovery of the capital investments needed to sustain the sector with an appropriate return on investment.

During the Soviet era, tariffs in the CSE/CIS countries were generally set at levels well below the long-term supply cost. The price structure was further distorted by cross-subsidies from industry and commercial operations to residential consumers. This pattern is still in place in a number of the countries in the region (see figure 6.2).

As a rule of thumb, the long-run marginal cost of generation will be 6.5–7.5 cents per kWh (excluding costs associated with transmission and distribution). This estimate is based on construction of a gas-fired combined cycle power plant and assumes a gas price of $250–$300 per thousand cubic meters.

In 2008 most CSE countries were covering the long-run marginal cost of generation (figure 6.2). As a result, utilities in these countries have been able to attract both foreign and domestic investors. In contrast, in many of the CIS countries, electricity tariffs did not appear to

FIGURE 6.2

Weighted-Average Residential and Nonresidential Electricity Tariffs in the Region, by Economy, 2008

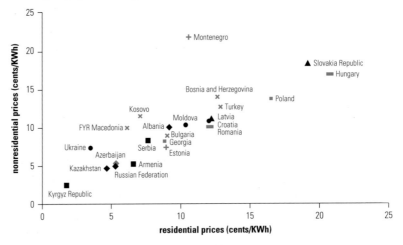

Source: Energy Regulators Region Association, tariff database 2009.

be adequate to cover long-run marginal costs, although in a number of these countries—notably Russia—domestic tariffs for gas were well below international parity levels and hence short-run marginal costs were substantially lower than in countries in which gas was priced at full international levels.

In most of the countries in the region, the tariff for residential customers was equal to or lower than the tariff for nonresidential customers, despite the fact that the cost of supplying residential customers is higher than that of supplying nonresidential customers. This indicates cross-subsidization.

Structuring the Energy Sector to Attract Investment

Unbundling the energy sector is the single most effective structural mechanism a government can use to increase transparency and competition within the sector. Vertical unbundling in the case of the power sector refers to the separation of generation, transmission, and distribution entities. Horizontal unbundling involves separating power generation companies with a view to deepening competition and separating distribution companies to support industry liberalization.

Experience in the region suggests that reform programs should be adapted to suit the specific conditions of each country. The degree of vertical and horizontal unbundling for one country may be different from that in another country; relevant factors to consider include system size, resource endowment, and institutional capacity to manage complex trading mechanisms (ESMAP 2006). In medium to large power markets with strong institutional capacity, full horizontal and vertical unbundling is generally preferred. For small markets, horizontal unbundling into small entities would generally not make sense, unless there are reasonable prospects for an open market with neighboring countries. However, some degree of vertical unbundling would help increase transparency of operations and facilitate both market growth and regional power trade.

Bearing this in mind, reform can be viewed in a broader sense as a means to improve the governance of the energy sector. By undertaking appropriate reforms, governments can create a commercially oriented environment that should attract capital inflows. Retaining a vertically integrated monopoly offers too many opportunities for noncommercial behavior that will be perceived by private investors as increasing risk.

There has been a widespread move toward sector unbundling of the power sectors in the region (figure 6.3). Only a few countries, such as

FIGURE 6.3

Horizontal and Vertical Unbundling in the Region's Electricity Markets, 2008

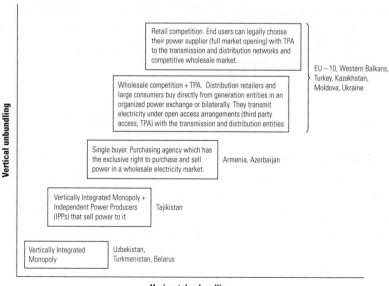

Source: World Bank staff.

Belarus, Turkmenistan, and Uzbekistan, still retain their state-owned vertically integrated power monopolies. However, despite significant progress in terms of market restructuring, there remain a number of obstacles to the operation of fully functional liberalized power markets, even in markets that have opened up both wholesale and retail competition. For example, the three largest generators control more than 70 percent of the generation capacity in the Czech Republic, Estonia, Latvia, Lithuania, the Slovak Republic, and Slovenia (all members of the EU10). In the retail market, concentration is even higher. Moving toward a more liberalized market structure in countries that have implemented only minimal reform and addressing the remaining obstacles for countries with more advanced reform programs are challenges that need to be addressed if appropriate levels of private sector investment are to be secured.

Addressing Affordability Concerns

One of the consequences of comprehensive energy sector reform is that the population will be expected to pay the full cost for the energy consumed. This is an issue for the poor in the region and one that requires appropriate mitigating measures. Energy prices need to be set at cost-recovery levels if investment is to take place to modernize old and build new capacity. But raising prices may push energy prices out of the reach of the poor and vulnerable. Household expenditure shares for energy continue to increase; the introduction of full cost-recovery pricing would make affordability a concern in many countries, particularly as poor households already devote a much larger share of expenditures to paying for energy than better-off households.

The contraction and transition of the region's economies in the late 1980s and early 1990s led to an impoverishment of the population of the region to such an extent that by 1998, nearly 21 percent—102 million people—were classified as poor (living on a daily income of $2.15 or less) (figure 6.4). Rising incomes have since dramatically reduced poverty by about 45 million poor and 38 million vulnerable. However, the current financial and economic crises have created the risk of higher poverty and vulnerability, especially in low-income countries.

In the past, governments in the region have used heat and power tariffs to industrial and commercial consumers to cross-subsidize residential tariffs, tolerated nonpayment of utility charges, and refrained from disconnecting nonpaying residential customers, especially for district heat supplies. These approaches are not sustainable, because

FIGURE 6.4

Population of the Region, by Poverty Status, 1998/99–2005/06

(millions)

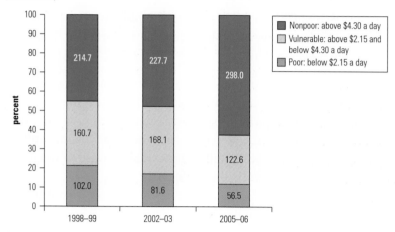

Source: Bank staff estimates.

the heat and power suppliers are unable to cover their costs and maintain financial viability. Some governments have also provided tariff discounts, free coal, or both to different classes of "privileged persons," such as pensioners, war veterans, people with disabilities, and retired coal miners. This approach, found in many CIS countries, is designed more to reward service than to reduce poverty. It does not generally help the unemployed and their families, its leakage of benefits to nonpoor can be very high, and it can suffer from high levels of billing abuse.

Four instruments have proved effective in aiding the poor: lifeline tariffs, burden limits, earmarked cash transfers, and nonearmarked cash transfers. The appropriateness of each instrument has to be evaluated with reference to the following criteria:

- *Coverage.* What percentage of the poor is reached by this instrument?
- *Targeting.* What percentage of the subsidy goes to the poor?
- *Predictability.* Can the poor be sure what they will receive and plan accordingly?
- *Price distortion.* Does the scheme cause price distortions and impose economic welfare costs on the system?
- *Administrative cost.* How expensive is the scheme to administer? How practical is it under country circumstances?
- *Target consumption.* How good is the scheme at ensuring that households achieve a minimum essential level of heat and power access?

- *Balanced approach*. How good is the scheme at balancing the financial viability needs of power, heat, and fuel supplies with the ability of consumers to pay?
- *Cross-subsidization*. Is subsidization taking place within a subsector (for example, power) or between subsectors (for example, between power and heat)?

Many countries operate more than one option simultaneously in an attempt to improve coverage and targeting. To protect the poor during and after tariff reform, this report recommends providing cash transfers to the poor as the preferred instrument and lifeline tariffs as a second best if meters are installed. Policymakers need to weigh the pros and cons of various schemes (table 6.4).

Other actions could also help mitigate the effects on poor households. These include the following:

- Ensuring access to electricity services and implementing service standards, such as 24-hour supply with steady voltage and frequency regulation
- Using medium-term tariff plans and phased adjustment of tariffs
- Enabling fuel switching to cheaper energy, such as gas for heating and cooking
- Promoting energy efficiency, such as better insulation of houses to reduce heat losses and the use of energy-efficient appliances and light bulbs.

Governments also need to address other social concerns. Energy production, including hydropower development, can have significant negative social impacts for local populations. The region's governments should bring their legislation, regulations, procedures, and practices in line with good international practices for social mitigation by ensuring that people affected by projects are fully informed and consulted regarding current energy activities and proposed new developments. They should give special attention to the needs of women, children, youth, and disadvantaged groups, adopting initiatives to mitigate potential social risks and ensure that these groups get a fair share of the employment, income, and other benefits generated by the energy sector.

TABLE 6.4

Benefits and Shortcomings of Various Social Mitigation Schemes for Tariff Increases

Mechanism	Benefits	Shortcomings
Nonearmarked cash transfers (social security and/or pension schemes)	Coverage depends on the ability and willingness of the poor to meet the eligibility criteria; it is the least distortionary of the utility subsidy mechanisms. There are no additional administrative requirements if a social assistance system is already in place; there is no financial burden for utilities or other (nonhousehold) consumers.	The targeting ratio of the poor is usually at a medium or low level; there is a significant fiscal cost.
Earmarked cash transfers (cash payments or vouchers to selected households for payment of a part of the utility bills, to ensure that the families meet a specified household income target)	The targeting ratio is relatively high; the net financial burden on utilities is low.	Coverage of the poor is highly uncertain and in most surveyed countries low. Transfers are administratively demanding.
Lifeline tariffs (tariff in which the lowest block of consumption is charged at a rate substantially lower than the average tariff)	Coverage of the poor is high; targeting ratio improves as the size of the initial block decreases. Benefits received are highly predictable, especially through a two-block life-line tariff. The scheme is simple to administer.	Because the poor tend to be underrepresented among those with utility connections, many would not benefit. Administration requires reliable (tamperproof) metering or a reasonable proxy (such as apartment size for heating) to estimate consumption; disciplined meter readers/controllers are needed. There is a significant burden on the budget, on the finances of the utility, and on other (industrial) consumers (if the cost is recovered through a higher industrial tariff).
Notional burden limits (system under which households pay a specified percentage of their household disposable income, above which payments are made by the government to the utility)	Benefits can be predicted with reasonable certainty; administrative costs are relatively low.	Coverage and targeting of the poor is usually relatively low, and there are heavy administrative burdens on the poor associated with its application. It is one of the most distortionary mechanisms of all utility subsidy mechanisms on the demand side. It is costly for the budget and requires a network of offices to administer.

Source: World Bank 2005.

Regional Cooperation and Trade: Examples in Southeastern Europe and Central Asia

Southeastern Europe

Regional cooperation is critical for Southeastern Europe, where many countries will likely rely on imports to close temporary supply shortfalls or on exports to improve the economics of developing new capacity in their small domestic power systems. If investment capacity lags, the sub-region may experience power deficits, becoming increasingly reliant on imports from outside. But the availability of enough imported power on affordable terms remains a question in view of the stresses facing most European countries.

Countries that plan to rely on gas-fired generation capacity must be confident that other countries will also follow this regional priority rather than pursue self-sufficiency in generating capacity based on nongas sources. But many Southeastern European countries have announced plans to build new generating capacity without a gas-fired component—not promising for gas supply infrastructure in the region.

Electricity trade in Southeastern Europe accounts for about 10 percent of final power demand in the region (15 percent, including trade with Greece and Turkey). The main exporters are Bosnia and Herzegovina, Bulgaria, and Romania. The other countries are net

TABLE A.1

Progress toward an Efficient Electricity Market in the Western Balkans

Economy	Directive 2003/54/EC[1]	Market structure	Wholesale market	Tariff reform affordability	Market integration
Albania	B	C	C	D	C
Bosnia and Herzegovina	B	C	C	D	C
Croatia	A	B	B	B	B
FYR Macedonia	B	C	C	D	C
Montenegro	B	C	C	D	C
Serbia	B	C	C	C	C
Kosovo	B	C	C	D	D

Source: Energy Community Secretariat 2007.

Note: A = all provisions are available; B = some provisions are missing; C = some provisions are available; D = bottlenecks to progress. The EU Directive on the creation of an integrated electricity market focuses on breaking up vertically integrated supply chains to allow competition in the power market, regulated third party access to the power network, coexistence of regulated and competitive components side by side, and freedom for eligible consumers to choose their suppliers. Directive 2003/54/EC

importers. Trade is typically on a short-term basis, characterized by limited competition, high transaction costs, and low flexibility in exploiting trading opportunities.

The countries of Southeastern Europe have established an integrated market in natural gas and electricity under the Energy Community Treaty. But progress toward an efficient market in the Western Balkans has been uneven (table A.1). Bulgaria and Romania have progressed much farther than countries in the Western Balkans. The Energy Community Treaty's requirements for the gas sector largely mirror those for electricity. They include (a) establishing an independent regulator, (b) unbundling different gas industry functions and legally separating transmission and distribution from other functions, (c) opening access to network and storage facilities, and (d) opening access to the gas market.

To support the development of the electricity market, the World Bank assessed the required investment in power generation. The Southeastern Europe Generation Investment Study was carried out in 2004–05 and updated in 2007 to account for large increases in fuel prices (box A.1).

Developing the region's gas supply infrastructure requires that countries include in their plans new gas-fired capacity on their territories or imported electricity based on gas-fired capacity in neighboring countries. The Energy Community Gas Ring concept will promote regional market integration, which is critical to developing substantial gas infrastructure in the region and helping its countries exploit others' choices for gas supply (box A.2). The capital cost is estimated at $1 billion, and the gas-fired power plants needed to secure an

---

BOX A.1
_____

The Southeastern Europe Generation Investment Study

The Generation Investment Study analyzed the least-cost means to meet forecast demand in Southeastern Europe by treating the region as one system, given the existing capital stock (which could potentially be rehabilitated or retired) and the opportunities for investment in new plants (lignite, gas-fired, hydropower, and nuclear). The study analyzed various planning scenarios to reflect different projections of development strategies, fuel costs, imports, environmental policies, and the like.

The updated study concluded that about 9,300 megawatts (MW) of generation capacity could be rehabilitated by 2020 in accordance with least-cost development, and partly completed and committed plants—including 2,320 MW of new nuclear power capacity in Bulgaria and Romania and 1,440 MW of new lignite-based plants in Bulgaria and Serbia—could be completed. The study identified 12,696 MW of new generation capacity required under the base scenario: 4,800 MW from local lignite in Kosovo, 2,500 MW from imported coal, and 2,100 MW from gas-fired, combined-cycle plants using imported gas. Too large for national power markets, many of these components (such as the Kosovo lignite-fired capacity) require a regional power market. The cost of the rehabilitation and new capacity is estimated at €16.7 billion (in 2006 prices).

Source: REBIS and GIS 2004; PwC Atkins MWH Consortium 2007.

BOX A.2
_____

Gasifying Southeastern Europe

The Ionian Adriatic pipeline, part of the broader Energy Community Gas Ring project, would connect the non-gasified markets of Albania, southern Croatia, and Montenegro. Linking to the trans-Adriatic pipeline, it would connect the Albanian, Greek, and Italian gas systems with gas from Russia, the Caspian Basin, and the Middle East. Branches of the Ionian pipeline would be developed at the same time as anchor power plants, along with pipeline trunks. Three power plants would anchor the €230 million investment, making it economic and bankable. The plants would be at the energy terminal of Fieri, in southern Albania; in the coastal city of Split, in southern Croatia; and in Podgorica, in Montenegro. But the prospects for these plants are uncertain, because they are not included in these countries' announced plans for generating capacity.

---

anchor load will cost $1.3–$2.3 billion. This infrastructure would be developed incrementally. The first stages would bring gas to new power stations in non-gasified areas on the Adriatic Coast, where power shortages constrain growth in tourism.

The big questions are whether new gas sources will be available to supply new demand and whether Russian and indigenous gas resources can continue to supply existing demand. Options for incremental new supply are gas through pipelines from the Russian Federation, the Caspian Basin, or Central and Eastern Europe and liquefied natural gas from North Africa and the Middle East. The most promising options are the following:

- Exporting Russian gas through Macedonia (although mountainous terrain increases cost)
- Linking to the Greek pipeline system (to carry Russian/ Caspian gas)
- Building liquefied natural gas facilities in Fieri (Albania), Krk (Croatia), or both[1]
- Constructing a trans-Adriatic pipeline (to carry Russian/ Caspian gas)
- Extending the Croatian pipeline through Hungary
- Backhauling gas from Italy, with Russian gas swaps
- Backhauling Revithoussa liquefied natural gas from Greece.

Which of these options will be developed depends on the assured availability of the gas; given uncertainties about availability, countries should not base their energy strategies on an assumption that any particular project will materialize. In practice, large external gas suppliers and consumers may make the choices subject to strong geopolitical rivalries between Russia and the European Union. Southeastern European countries should be ready to exploit those choices, finding ways to advance their interests in the presence of large external influences.

Given the high capital intensity of pipeline projects, other key issues are whether there will be enough investment in infrastructure to bring the gas to market and whether that investment will come soon enough to displace coal and oil products. A technical feasibility study for the Energy Community Gas Ring shows that transmission charges would have to be 11 percent higher if only half the required anchor load were in place when the pipeline was commissioned and half added over the next 10 years, compared with the charges if all the anchor load were present at commissioning (Economic Consulting Associates Ltd., Penspen, EIHP, and Untergrundspeicher und Geotechnologie System GmbH, 2008). The added charge would be 30 percent if only a third of the anchor load were in place at commissioning and the rest added over the following 15 years.

Central Asia

Central Asia has considerable potential for exporting energy, both within its boundaries and beyond (figures A.1 and A.2). But the prospects for realizing this potential are uncertain because of the long history of distrust among the region's countries and their lack of institutional and financial capacity. The Central Asian Regional Economic Cooperation (CAREC) and other regional forums supported by international institutions and donors may hold some promise for overcoming those obstacles.

Central Asian states have traditionally depended on one another for energy and water. For example, hydropower plants in the Kyrgyz Republic and Tajikistan operate on schedules that suit crop irrigation. These upstream states release more water in warmer seasons, when the downstream states need it for irrigation, in exchange receiving gas, coal, and electricity imports to alleviate their cold season shortages and agreements to purchase the surplus electricity from warmer months.

The arrangement has not always worked well in practice. In 1998, Kazakhstan, the Kyrgyz Republic, and Uzbekistan concluded a long-term framework agreement on the water and energy resources of the Syr Darya River. Tajikistan later signed as well. But the agreement did not spur adherence to commitments. The arrangements weakened when Uzbekistan's interest in importing electricity in the summer declined and it insisted on cash for its gas, rather than electricity and the benefits of water storage and seasonal release. Because the demand patterns in Central Asia coincide (winter peak, summer off-peak), there is little market for surplus hydropower in the summer.

There is no framework agreement on water and energy exchange in place for the Amu Darya River, shared by Tajikistan, Turkmenistan, and Uzbekistan. Uzbekistan expressed concern about the planned expansion of Tajik hydroelectric production on the Vakhsh River, a tributary of the Amu Darya, fearing that it will restrict water flow into Uzbekistan and enable Tajikistan to block the Vakhsh, which provides a quarter of the Amu Darya flow. Uzbekistan expanded its reservoir capacity to reduce vulnerability to the upstream countries.

Meanwhile, Uzbekistan monetized gas trade with its neighbors and, like Gazprom, raised the price of its natural gas considerably in a series of increases, from $42 per thousand cubic meters in 2005 to $240 in 2009.

These price hikes encouraged the Kyrgyz Republic and Tajikistan to look to hydropower, not gas, for their energy needs. They also made these states reluctant to depend on downstream suppliers'

FIGURE A.1

Central Asia's Surplus Electricity to Peak in the 2010s

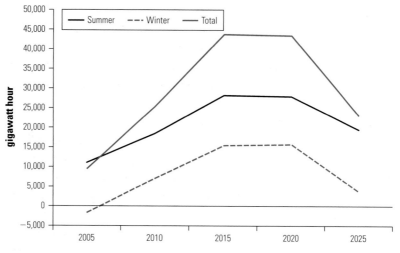

Source: World Bank staff projections.

FIGURE A.2

Tajikistan's Energy Exports to Rise, Especially Electricity

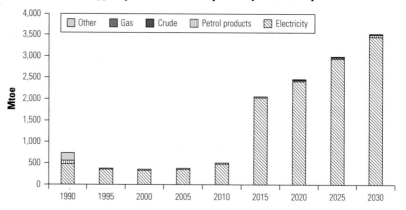

Source: IEA historical data, staff projections. Data for 1990–2005 are from IEA 2008a and 2008b; data for 2010–2030 are World Bank staff projections.

willingness to sell fuels during political strains or disputes over payment.[2] Without agreements on electricity export or monetization of the benefits of water storage, the Kyrgyz Republic and Tajikistan lean toward solutions that increase their energy self-sufficiency. Both states, especially Tajikistan, hope to export hydroelectric power to other clients (Afghanistan, China, Iran, Pakistan, and others). They therefore prefer to develop water storage and release schedules for those exports rather than for the needs of downstream states.

Afghanistan, the Kyrgyz Republic, Pakistan, and Tajikistan are developing a Central Asia Regional Electricity Market (CASAREM) to develop electricity trade through projects and concomitant investments, underpinned by the necessary institutional and legal arrangements. The idea is to exploit Central Asia's surplus hydropower in summer to meet high and growing demand in South Asia and monetize it. The countries have intensified cooperation since 2005, both among themselves and with international financial institutions and bilateral donors. It is envisaged that other countries could join as trade expands.

Sustainable regional cooperation in Central Asia on energy requires two things: regional cooperation and government willingness to create business climates that attract the huge investments required. These conditions are vital for ensuring adherence to contract commitments (including payments), stopping side deals that undermine investment viability, and countering the prevailing non-performance of obligations. In turn, the cashflow needed to make contract payments will be available only if service providers remain financially solvent and are able to charge prices that reflect costs. Today, both conditions are absent.

A key change will be adoption of a more commercial approach to structuring and regulating energy markets. Because markets develop best with many buyers and sellers that can trade freely among themselves, these countries should separate their energy transmission businesses into entities that are independent of producers and distributors and allow traders to access these facilities on nondiscriminatory, regulated terms. Kazakhstan and the Kyrgyz Republic have already done this, but Tajikistan and Uzbekistan have yet to start (World Bank 2008b).

The countries of the sub-region need to conclude agreements for exploiting the international water resources of their many rivers. These agreements need an equitable basis for sharing benefits, through the construction and operation of large hydropower storage plants. The agreements should incorporate a multiyear (10 years at least) perspective and an explicit recognition of downstream states' obligation to pay for the annual and multiyear water storage services that upstream countries provide at considerable economic cost.

These agreements will be subject to external geopolitical influences, especially from Russia, the European Union, China, and South Asia. Strategic objectives are diverse. Russia has projects to export oil and gas to China and other countries and is helping Kazakhstan with its oil exports to China. The European Union focuses on facilitating Central Asian oil and gas exports to Europe. China invests in developing production in Central Asia and imports from the region. South Asia is becoming a potential market for major electricity exports from Tajikistan.

Notes

1. Uncertainty faces the liquefied natural gas facilities along the Adriatic Coast, including in Krk and Fieri. Competing projects are under development on the Italian Adriatic coast, in Rovigo (Panigaglia), and Brindisi. Agreement may not be imminent given the many parties involved—six foreign companies and three national in Croatia for example—and the environmental considerations.
2. Uzbekistan has cut gas shipments to the Kyrgyz Republic and Tajikistan because of nonpayment. It has also cut supplies for political reasons (in response to the Kyrgyz Republic's acceptance of refugees from Andijan in 2005, for example). In the past it has also blocked the transit of electricity from the Kyrgyz Republic and Turkmenistan to Tajikistan.

References

ADEME (Agence de l'Environnement et de la Maîtrise de l'Energie [French Environment and Energy Management Agency]), and IEEA (Intelligent Energy Executive Agency). 2007. *Evaluation of Energy Efficiency in the EU-15: Indicators and Policies*. Paris.

Aslanyan, Garegin. 2006. *Russia's Energy Efficiency and Indicators*. Presentation at Introduction to Energy Indicators Workshop, International Energy Agency, Paris, April.

Baugh, Kimberly E., Christopher D. Elvidge, Edward H. Erwin, Ara T. Howard, Cristina Milesi, Dee W. Pack, and Benjamin T. Tuttle. 2007. *A Twelve-Year Record of National and Global Gas Flaring Volumes Estimated Using Satellite Data*. Final report to the World Bank, May 30.

British Petroleum. 2008. *BP Statistical Review of World Energy*. London.

———. 2009. *BP Statistical Review of World Energy*. London.

Cambridge Energy Research Associates. 2008.

Cardais, A. S. 2008. "Investment: Seeing the Green Light: The Emergence of a Green Energy Market Central and Eastern Europe." In TOL (Transitions Online) Special Report *Energy*. Prague.

CEC (Commission of the European Communities). 2007. *Communication from the Commission to the European Council and the European Parliament: An Energy Policy for Europe*. Brussels.

EBRD (European Bank for Reconstruction and Development). 2008. *Transition Report*. London.

Economic Consulting Associates, Ltd., Penspen, Energy Institute Hrvoje Požar (EIHP), and Untergrundspeicher und Geotechnologie System GmbH. 2008. *South East Europe: Regional Gasification Study*. London.

EIA (Energy Information Administration). 2005.

———. 2007. *International Energy Outlook 2007*. May. Washington, DC.

Energy Charter Secretariat. 2008. *In-Depth Review of the Energy Efficiency Policy of Bulgaria*. Brussels.

Energy Community Secretariat. 2007. "Implementation of the Treaty (Status as of November 2007): Electricity." Presentation to the Third Ministerial Council meeting, Belgrade, December 18.

ESMAP (Energy Sector Management Assistance Program). 2006. *Reforming Power Markets in Developing Countries: What Have We Learned?* World Bank, Washington, DC.

European Commission. 2008a. *Package of Implementation Measures for the EU's Objectives on Climate Change and Renewable Energy for 2020*. Brussels.

———. 2008b. *Proposal for a Directive of the European Parliament and of the Council on the energy performance of buildings*. Brussels.

PCF Energy. 2007. *Using Russia's Associated Gas: Prepared for the Global Gas Flaring Reduction Partnership and the World Bank*. [http://siteresources. worldbank.org/INTGGFR/Resources/pfc_energy_report.pdf]

IEA (International Energy Agency). 2005. 30 *Key Energy Trends in the IEA and Worldwide*. Paris.

———. 2006a. *Energy Technology Perspectives*. Paris.

———. 2006b. *Optimizing Russian Natural Gas: Reform and Climate Change*. Paris.

———. 2006c. *World Energy Outlook 2006 Edition*. Paris.

———. 2007a. *World Energy Outlook 2007 Edition*. Paris.

———. 2007b. *CO$_2$ Emissions from Fuel Combustion 2007 Edition*. Paris.

———. 2008a. *Energy Balances of OECD Countries 2008 Edition*. Paris.

———. 2008b. *Energy Balances of non-OECD Countries 2008 Edition*. Paris.

———. 2008c. *Energy Efficiency Requirements in Building Codes, Energy Efficiency Policies for New Buildings*. Paris.

———. 2008d. *Energy in the Western Balkans: The Path to Reform and Reconstruction*. Paris.

IFC (International Finance Corporation). 2007. *Banking on Sustainability*. Washington, DC.

International Herald Tribune. 2006. "A Side Door to Russia's Oil Fields." July 13.

IPCC (Intergovernmental Panel on Climate Change). 2007. *Climate Change 2007: The Physical Science Basis, Summary for Policymakers*. Working Group I Contribution to the Intergovernmental Panel on Climate Change, Fourth Assessment Report. Geneva.

McKinsey Global Institute. 2007. *Curbing Energy Demand Growth: The Energy Productivity Opportunity*. London.

McKinsey & Company. 2009. *Pathways to a Low-Carbon Economy – Version 2 of the Global Greenhouse Gas Abatement Cost Curve*.

Parry, Ian, W. H., and William A. Pizer. 2007. *Emissions Trading versus CO₂ Taxes versus Standards*. Washington, DC: Resources for the Future.

Point Carbon. 2007. *Carbon 2007: A New Climate for Carbon Trading*. Copenhagen.

PwC Atkins MWH Consortium, and Development of Power Generation in Southeastern Europe. 2007. *Update of Generation Investment Study*. Final Report, January 31.

REBIS (Regional Balkans Infrastructure Study-Electricity), and GIS (Generation Investment Study). 2004. Final Report, December 31. London.

Simmons, Daniel, and Isabel Murray. 2007. *Russian Gas: Will There Be Enough Investment?* Enerpub (Energy Publisher), September 25. http://www.energypublisher.com/article.asp?id=11200

Stern, Nicholas. 2006. *The Stern Review: The Economics of Climate Change*. London.

World Bank. 2003. *Croatia Energy Efficiency Project*. Washington, DC.

———. 2004. "Options for Designing a Green Investment Scheme for Bulgaria." Europe and Central Asia Region, Infrastructure and Energy Department and Carbon Finance Unit, Washington, DC.

———. 2005. *Azerbaijan: Issues and Options Associated with Energy Sector Reform*. Europe and Central Asia Region, Infrastructure and Energy Department, Washington, DC.

———. 2006. *Infrastructure in Europe and Central Asia: Approaches to Sustainable Services*. Washington, DC: World Bank.

———. 2007a. "*People and Power—Electricity Sector Reforms and the Poor in Europe and Central Asia*". Washington, DC: World Bank.

———. 2007b. *World Development Indicators*. Washington, DC: World Bank.

———. 2008a. "*Rosneft Gas Flaring Reduction Project.*" Project Information Document. Washington DC: World Bank.

———. 2008b. *Central Asian Regional Economic Cooperation. Strategy for Regional Cooperation in the Energy Sector of CAREC Countries*. April. Europe and Central Asia Region, Washington, DC.

———. 2008c. "Climate Change for Development Professionals." Presentation during Sustainable Development Network Week, Febrauary 19th–29th, Washington, DC.

World Bank, and GEF (Global Environmental Facility). 2006. *Post-Implementation Impact Assessment—Poland Efficient Lighting*. Washington, DC.

World Bank, and IFC (International Finance Corporation). 2008. *Energy Efficiency in Russia: Untapped Reserves*. Washington, DC.

World Energy Council. 2007. *Survey of Energy Resources*. London.

World Wind Energy Association. 2009. *World Wind Energy Report 2008*. Bonn.

Index

Boxes, figures, notes, and tables are indicated with *b*, *f*, *n*, and *t* following the page number.